WHY CEOs FAIL

WHY CEOs FAIL

The 11 Behaviors That Can Derail
Your Climb to the Top
—and How to Manage Them

DAVID L. DOTLICH
PETER C. CAIRO

Forewords by
Ram Charan and
Robert Hogan

JOSSEY-BASS
A Wiley Imprint
www.josseybass.com

Published by Jossey-Bass
A Wiley Imprint
989 Market Street, San Francisco, CA 94103-1741   www.josseybass.com

Jossey-Bass books and products are available through most bookstores. To contact Jossey-Bass directly call our Customer Care Department within the U.S. at 800-956-7739, outside the U.S. at 317-572-3986, or fax 317-572-4002.

Jossey-Bass also publishes its books in a variety of electronic formats. Some content that appears in print may not be available in electronic books.

Library of Congress Cataloging-in-Publication Data

Dotlich, David L. (David Landreth), 1950-
   Why CEOs fail : the 11 behaviors that can derail your climb to the top—and how to manage them / by David L. Dotlich, Peter C. Cairo.
       p. cm.
Includes bibliographical references and index.
   ISBN 0-7879-6763-7 (alk. paper)
   1. Leadership. 2. Chief executive officers. 3. Executive ability. 4. Organizational effectiveness. I. Cairo, Peter C., 1948- II. Title.
   HD57.7.D683 2003
   658.4'2—dc21   2003002307

Printed in the United States of America
FIRST EDITION
HB Printing   V10006159_120418

CONTENTS

To all of the leaders we have worked with who have opened themselves to learning and to us, and in the process created this book.

According to David Dotlich and Peter Cairo, leadership failure is a behavioral phenomenon. In other words, it doesn't just happen. It's not just the result of a downturn in the economy or other events over which we have little control.

Instead, leaders fail because of who they are and how they act in certain situations. Especially under stress, they respond with a pattern of behavior that can sabotage their jobs and careers. They rely on a specific way of thinking, speaking, and acting that ultimately causes them to fail. Many times, they're not even aware that their behaviors have become reflexive.

This book makes a significant contribution to the literature of leadership, in that it identifies eleven behavioral patterns that can result in failure and suggests how CEOs and other leaders can learn to manage these patterns.

This is a book based on experience. The authors have worked with many of the world's top executives and organizations for years, and they write from their keen perception of human behavior in organizational settings. They understand both why leaders fail and why they succeed, and this understanding is evident in the stories they tell and in their useful suggestions.

Dotlich and Cairo have also drawn on the work of psychologist Robert Hogan, whose research about "leadership derailers" is extensive and perceptive. As the authors readily acknowledge in the following pages, this research has provided them with insights about the behaviors they've observed.

Why do CEOs and other leaders fail? Different authors have different answers, but here you'll find eleven provocative reasons that will cause you to look at failure from a fresh perspective and take steps to prevent your own potential derailers from interfering with your leadership effectiveness.

Dallas, Texas   Ram Charan
February 2003

Leadership is the most important topic in the managerial sciences. Although Marxist-inspired theorists argue that leaders are created by historical circumstances, more psychologically oriented people believe that leadership is a function of the characteristics of individuals. This book is based on a psychological view of leadership; although such an assumption seems commonsensical, it has been the topic of furious academic debate over the years.

Having decided that leadership is the function of individual characteristics, the next question is, What are the characteristics that define leadership? Here is where matters begin to get seriously murky. The published literature on leadership is immense—actually overwhelming—and it is growing daily. This literature falls neatly into two camps; I refer to them as the Troubadour Tradition and the Academic Tradition. The Troubadour Tradition is by far the largest. It consists of such amiable works of pop fiction as *Leadership Lessons of Genghis Khan*, *Leadership Lessons of Jesus Christ*, and *Leadership Lessons of Abraham Lincoln*. It also consists of the opinions and score-settling reminiscences of countless former CEOs. From an empirical perspective, these works are high on entertainment value but low on truth value, and we can derive few defensible generalizations from them. On the other hand, the Academic Tradition contains many, many empirical nuggets, little gems such as "Leaders tend to be slightly taller than their constituencies." This is a valid statistical generalization but one that clearly doesn't apply to Admiral Horatio Nelson (the hero of the battle of Trafalgar, who saved England from French domination), Napoleon Bonaparte (the wannabe dominator), Winston Churchill (who saved England from German domination), or even America's own Jimmy Carter. From the perspective of a (nonacademic) layperson trying to understand leadership, the Academic Tradition has two problems: many of its insights are relatively trivial, and few of the insights replicate—there is little agreement across empirical studies regarding the defining characteristics of leadership.

So what do we know about leadership that is actually the case? The answer depends on how we define leadership, which is another vexed issue. My preference for resolving such definitional issues is to turn to the study of human origins (for a superb introduction, see Christopher Boehm's 1999 book, *Hierarchy in the Forest*). People evolved as group-living animals. The groups were in competition with other groups, and other groups sought constantly to appropriate the resources of any particular group. If a particular group was taken over, the males were killed, eaten, or otherwise dispersed, and they usually disappeared from the gene pool. Individual fitness depended on the survival of the group, leadership was a key to group survival, and this holds a key to how we should define leadership. *Leadership concerns the capacity to build and maintain a high-performing team, and leadership should be evaluated in terms of the performance of the team.*

So what do we know, in a reliable way, about leadership, defined in terms of the ability to build and maintain a team? I believe we know three things. First, as outlined in Jim Kouzes and Barry Posner's *Leadership Challenge* (2002), competent leaders are perceived as having four characteristics in common:

- They have integrity—they keep their word, they don't play favorites, they tell the truth.

- They are decisive—they make sound, defensible decisions in a timely fashion.

- They are competent—they are obviously good at some aspects of the business.

- They are visionary—they can explain why the team's activity is important and how that activity contributes to the future well-being of the team.

The second thing we know is that leaders of great companies not only project integrity, decisiveness, competence, and vision, they are also quite humble and phenomenally persistent: see Jim Collins's *Good to Great* (2002).

The third thing that we know for a fact about leaders is that perhaps two-thirds of the people currently in leadership positions in the Western world will fail; they will then be fired, demoted, or kicked upstairs. The most common reason for their failure will be their inability to build or maintain a team. Their inability to build a team will be a function of certain dysfunctional dispositions, interpersonal tendencies that are usually invisible during job interviews or assessment center exercises. These tendencies usually become apparent when people are under pressure or when they let down their guard. Moreover, there is considerable consensus regarding the nature of these dysfunctional dispositions. They reliably fall into eleven categories, and they can be assessed with considerable fidelity.

The present book is an important, even fundamental, contribution to the leadership literature because it says some things that are empirically true, and it says some things that are pragmatically important. The book concerns common tendencies of leaders that will derail their careers and in so doing will cause considerable damage to the organizations where they work. Anyone who is concerned with organizational effectiveness in general and leadership in particular will find this book invaluable.

Amelia Island, Florida   Robert Hogan
February 2003

Which of the following answers is the best explanation for why CEOs fail:

a. Not responding effectively to a competitor's successful new technology, product, or service.

b. Being unable to define a clear vision or direction for the business.

c. Failing to execute a brilliant strategy.

d. Communicating poorly with the Board of Directors.

e. Losing talented people and being unable to replace them.

If you answered yes to any of these choices, you are partially correct. Chief executive officers, as well as other leaders, fail because they do things—or don't do things—that cost their organizations a lot of money, create negative publicity, undermine their competitive edge, or drive away good people. But on another level, these answers only explain the explicit reason for failure and not the underlying causes that may have prompted leaders to do the wrong things.

CEOs and other top executives are almost always bright, savvy, highly experienced business leaders with terrific track records. But the average tenure of CEOs in major companies today is growing increasingly shorter. Magazine covers flaunt stories of fallen idols. In a very short period, CEOs have gone from "most admired" status to "least trusted." Why do such obviously talented leaders also make poor decisions, alienate key people, miss opportunities, and overlook obvious trends and developments?

As coaches of many CEOs and faculty for senior executive leadership programs around the world, we found this question troubling, especially in light of the many CEO failures in recent years. Our backgrounds (Dotlich is a former executive at Honeywell International and Cairo a former professor at Columbia University) have made us well aware of leadership theory, and we have witnessed how flawed strategies and other cognitive missteps had hurt CEOs and their companies. We have also seen that many failures had to do with obvious mistakes in executing reasonable strategies. Historically, many CEOs who made suddenly irreversible mistakes were considered strong leaders before their blunders. Had they experienced a sudden, momentary loss of judgment that caused them to err? Or was it something else?

Something else seemed likely. After all, most CEO failures aren't the result of insufficient intelligence. Generally, they happen when smart and well-intentioned leaders act in illogical, idiosyncratic, or irrational ways. Reading over case histories of company failures, you ask yourself, "How could the CEO not see that he needed to act immediately?" or "Why in the world didn't she grasp that the company couldn't survive pursuing that strategy?" or even, "Why didn't he know what was going on?" These failed leaders might have been able to save their careers if they had applied simple logic and common sense to the situations they faced.

Many of these leaders sabotaged themselves, albeit unconsciously. They had the intellect, skills, and experience to lead their companies through whatever challenges they encountered, yet for some reason they didn't do so. Something derailed their careers.

Something that was integral to who they were, both as people and as leaders, and that operated beneath their awareness.

We've found that CEOs, as well as all leaders, are vulnerable to eleven *derailers*—deeply ingrained personality traits that affect their leadership style and actions. The odds are that you possess at least one of these traits. For instance, you may be brilliant at analysis, and this analytical reflex has helped your company avoid the mistakes that competing companies have made. At the same time, your penchant for analysis may become warped when you're under stress. You become so analytical that you freeze when you should be taking action. When you should be deciding, you're still analyzing.

This drive to analyze overrides common sense. From your perspective, though, more analysis makes perfect sense. This trait is hardwired into you, and it's difficult to take a step back and realize that what is at times a strength has become a leadership derailer. You honestly don't see what you're doing wrong—after all, it's the same thing you have done successfully for years—and failure blindsides you.

The good news is that this failure can be prevented. When you learn to identify and manage these derailers, you can spot failure coming a long way off and take the steps necessary to keep it from hurting your career or your company. We're going to introduce you to these eleven derailers, but first we'd like to share how the breakthrough efforts of a few individuals inspired the ideas and tools you'll find in the following pages.

Learning About Failure

Robert Hogan, an industrial psychologist and professor, has done groundbreaking research on how leaders' "dark sides" can derail their careers and cause negative consequences for their organizations. His research on the derailers, grounded in earlier work on derailment at the Center for Creative Leadership and what we know about the structure of personalities, gave us a new framework that allowed us to think about why leaders fail. Partnering with Professor Hogan, we've put his model into practice and have adapted his findings into a special leadership assessment tool and report titled the CDR International Derailment Report, which we've administered to thousands of senior executives in major companies throughout the world. This book reflects the results.

Ram Charan has also influenced our work. Charan, a brilliant strategist, consultant, and author, and a former Harvard Business School professor, teaches in many of our leadership programs, and his insights about CEO failure and how it is linked to poor execution have been extremely useful in our efforts on behalf of clients. It was his *Fortune* magazine cover story a few years ago that gave us the impetus to do this book. The story explored the reasons for leadership failure, identifying the way many CEOs failed because they couldn't manage people relationships, understand stakeholder needs, and take other steps necessary to get things done. In our conversations with Charan, we kept returning to the question of *why*. Why do these otherwise highly talented CEOs have such difficulty getting the right things done correctly? Why do leaders who genuinely want to do the right thing end up doing the wrong thing? Charan, Hogan, and many of our clients agreed with our assessment that the bedrock cause lay beneath the surface—that many leaders unknowingly diminish their ability to execute.

Third, Daniel Goleman's groundbreaking work on emotional intelligence has helped reinforce our thesis that failure often has more to do with who people are than with what they know or how bright they are. Goleman's observation that managing negative impulses is a key to success dovetails with our finding that the most successful leaders are those who learn to manage their derailers.

When we founded CDR International a number of years ago, we focused on the people side of leadership. Since then, we have taught or coached thousands of senior executives in many functions, industries, countries, and cultures. Our belief, then as now, was that most leaders succeed or fail based on how well they work with others and how well they understand themselves. Putting this belief into practice, however, was initially a challenge. The work of researchers like Robert Hogan, Ram Charan, and Daniel Goleman greatly facilitated our efforts. At the very least, they reinforced our view that we were on to something. As we started coaching different leaders, we developed an approach that drew heavily on Hogan's work on derailers. Over time, we refined our approach to the point that we could help leaders anticipate what their vulnerabilities were and how and where they might emerge. In some cases we have helped leaders regain their effectiveness in the aftermath of significant failure. When coaching CEOs and other top executives, we've found that the vast majority of them do not receive adequate feedback or confrontation to help them understand their own personalities. Once they do, they are capable of adjusting their behaviors in ways that lead to increased success. With self-awareness and some easy-to-use tools, you can do the same thing.

Looking Beneath the Surface:
Understanding the Way Derailers Work

Here are the eleven derailers we have consistently found in senior leaders and CEOs, and which you will learn about in this book:

- Arrogance: You're right and everybody else is wrong.

- Melodrama: You always grab the center of attention.

- Volatility: Your mood swings drive business swings.

- Excessive Caution: The next decision you make may be your first.

- Habitual Distrust: You focus on the negatives.

- Aloofness: You disengage and disconnect.

- Mischievousness: Rules are made to be broken.

- Eccentricity: It's fun to be different just for the sake of it.

- Passive Resistance: Your silence is misinterpreted as agreement.

- Perfectionism: Get the little things right even if the big things go wrong.

- Eagerness to Please: Winning the popularity contest matters most.

Although you may see these derailers and immediately think you know which ones (or maybe all) apply to you, most people need the detailed information and tools each chapter provides to make an accurate self-diagnosis. For now, don't worry about which ones describe you; just keep the following points in mind.

First, and most important, derailers emerge most commonly under stress, but what's stressful for one person isn't stressful for another. Some people find deadlines stressful while others feel tremendous pressure when they have nothing to do. Stressful situations can involve anything from trying to take advantage of a major opportunity like an acquisition to changing jobs and adapting to a new culture. Change frequently causes stress, though some people thrive on change. The key, of course, is figuring out what kinds of stress you're vulnerable to and what triggers your derailers.

Second, the goal of this book is *not* to eliminate derailers. In fact, you can't—they are part of your personality. They haven't suddenly emerged ten or twenty years into your career. They've been with you from the start, only they may not have had significant negative consequences earlier. Sometimes it takes years for leaders to encounter situations or people that catalyze their derailers. Until then, their mischievous or eccentric qualities may even be viewed favorably while the negative side of the traits remains dormant. In some instances, too, organizations can overlook or even reinforce a top executive's negative characteristics. No doubt, many people at Enron were aware of Jeff Skilling's inflated view of himself. Recent articles have described Enron as possessing a culture of arrogance. As long as the company did well, however, people chose to deny the aspects of Skilling's leadership style that ultimately derailed him. In fact, it was probably easy to overlook them because his great confidence and ego also contributed to Enron's spectacular success. When things went wrong, though, these behaviors were magnified because they were part of what contributed to the company's spectacular fall, and in hindsight could be seen as even hindering its success. The goal of this book is to help leaders of all types understand their own derailers, determine under what circumstances they can occur, and learn ways to manage them.

Third, some of the most effective and successful leaders we know have multiple derailers. We're going to emphasize this point throughout the book: some derailers are both strengths and weaknesses. Until arrogance leads to derailment, a leader may be seen as extremely self-confident. It is only when self-confidence goes over the edge to arrogance that trouble strikes. Every trait has a positive side that helps people achieve success. It's only when you are unaware of the trait, deny its existence, or fail to see its downside that you run into problems.

Fourth, be aware that the average person has two or three derailers. While we've worked with people who have had many more and a few who seemed to lack any of them, the odds are that some will fit you perfectly. You should also be aware that you may have derailers that seem like the opposite of one another. For instance, you may ask yourself "How can I be eager to please and arrogant at the same time?" or "How can I be both aloof and melodramatic?" These apparent contradictions do sometimes occur. The explanation is that personality is complex and often contradictory. Moreover, different people and situations can bring out different behaviors. For instance, your desire to please others may emerge when dealing with bosses, boards, or customers and your tendency to exhibit arrogance during interactions with direct reports.

Why CEOs Derail More Than Other Leaders

This book could just as easily have been called "Why Leaders Fail" since these derailers apply to everyone. We chose CEOs, however, because they are symbols of leadership, and their stories of failure—of which there have been many recently—make fascinating reading. They provide a lens through which we can see how derailers can hurt the career of anyone—but at the top levels of companies derailers have much greater consequences. In other words, if they can cause a CEO to fail, they can cause any executive to self-destruct. Because we coach many CEOs, we also have some insights about the position and both how failure happens and how it's avoided. We will, however, include a number of stories about non-CEO leaders so you'll see how the derailment process is the same no matter what your title might be. As we're sure you're aware, failure can happen at every level of the organization.

Perhaps a more salient point, though, is that CEOs are more vulnerable than other leaders to these derailers. This is due, in part, to the pressures that confront the leader at the top of the pyramid. Being in the spotlight, feeling responsible for the careers of thousands of employees, dealing with intense pressure for short-term results while investing in the long term, leading in an era of incredible speed and complexity—all of this can activate derailers.

In addition, the higher you go in an organization, the less likely other people are to tell you about your failure-producing characteristics. CEOs' jokes are funnier, their insights are brighter, and they are routinely considered the fount of all wisdom. Direct reports are reluctant to mention to their chief executives that their arrogance is stifling, or that they're turning minor problems into big melodramas. This insulation from honest feedback usually prevents top leaders from being aware of the traits that are hurting them and their organizations.

How to Use This Book

This book is meant to be used. As we tell our coaching clients, our goal is not just to give you insights about why you do what you do. This is not the equivalent to years of therapy where you finally understand why you're a workaholic—perhaps the therapist helps you recall that your parents subtly demeaned you when you were a child—but you don't have a clue about how to stop this destructive behavior.

Each chapter is devoted to a single derailer and contains relevant anecdotes, diagnostic tools, and management actions. We've included public stories of CEOs who have failed as well as anecdotes of many well-known CEOs we've personally worked with—but we have changed the names of the latter, for reasons that will become obvious as you read the book. This parallel structure is purposeful, making the derailers easier to understand and the information easier to use.

Readers will come at this book from different leadership positions as well as different experiences with failure. Some may be senior executives who have tasted failure and know it well—while others may be senior leaders but haven't yet failed in a major way. Whoever you are, and whatever your position, this book can help. You can use it to rebound from failure and avoid making the same mistake twice or you can use it to prevent failure. By identifying your derailers and taking the steps necessary to get them under control, you can increase your leadership effectiveness.

Be aware, too, of the natural tendency to focus your attention on chapters that are devoted to *your* derailers. This is fine, in that you want to pay special attention to your personal vulnerabilities. At the same time, however, don't ignore the other derailers. All of them may be relevant, in one way or another. More significantly, understanding all the derailers will make you a better leader because you may see some of these traits in others—your direct reports, boss, colleagues, customers, and suppliers. With this knowledge, you can be sensitive to derailment triggers in your direct reports and coach them during the stressful periods. You can see what may be behind the puzzling behavior of your peers and those above you in the organization. You can arm yourself with the prescriptive information necessary to help people manage these potentially destructive behaviors.

Don't Be Reluctant to Take a Walk on the Dark Side

Writers from Aristotle to Shakespeare to recent political commentators have explored the dark side of personality and leadership. It's a natural impulse to wonder about our negative impulses as leaders, to investigate why we take actions that hurt others, ourselves, and our organizations. At the same time, this dark side is often considered taboo. We live in a celebrity culture where leaders seem to be expected to be perfect. The traditional notion of leaders, especially CEOs, as heroic figures still exists in many corporate cultures, and we don't like to admit that they have flaws, that the traits that make them special can also catalyze failure.

When leaders become icons—which is what they sometimes become when they're the subjects of magazine cover stories and enjoy lifestyles often very different from the majority of those who work for them—it seems heretical to criticize them. We want leaders to protect us and provide us with security, and they can't do this if they're flawed in any way. Sometimes we actually contribute unwittingly to these heroic myths.

It's essential to abandon this thinking. In our earlier book, *Unnatural Leadership*, we made the point that people can be great leaders but fallible human beings. In fact, most of the stories we tell are about good people who were trying to do the right thing but were blindsided by their dark side. Rather than deny their flaws, leaders need to accept and understand them. Those who don't—who pretend to be the perfect leader—greatly increase the odds that derailers will strike . . . and that they'll strike sooner rather than later.

You may be reluctant to look at your leadership flaws. Being self-critical or admitting your weaknesses is not how you were trained to be a leader. We know many leaders who equate honest self-scrutiny with insecurity, weakness, and looking back rather than looking forward. But it's how you'll succeed as a leader. Awareness of your derailers doesn't mean you have to dwell on how "bad" you are. Instead, it frees up your strengths. When you learn to manage your self-destructive traits, you allow your strengths to emerge.

You don't have to join the rapidly growing ranks of leaders who failed. Our greatest leaders, both in business and politics, have always been fallible. No matter what your fallibilities might be, you don't have to let them derail you or your organization. The key is accepting rather than denying your all-too-human flaws.

CHAPTER ONE

Arrogance

You're Right and
Everybody Else Is Wrong

I f Othello were CEO of Enron and Oedipus Rex in charge of WorldCom, they might well have made the same mistakes as Jeff Skilling and Bernie Ebbers. In tragedies both ancient and modern, leaders fall because of arrogance. Defined as "excessive pride" and inflated views of self-worth, arrogance routinely derails the best and the brightest. It thrives on success, confidence, and ego, and if you have plenty of any of these, beware! Many current and former CEOs, such as Gary Wendt, Martha Stewart, Durk Jager, and Robert Horton, have been described as arrogant, and that perception contributed to their failure in the top jobs.

One of the toughest balancing acts in the leadership business is between confidence and too much confidence. If you're going to succeed as a leader, you need to have confidence in your abilities. If you fail as a leader, you may have too much confidence. This oversimplifies the concept of arrogance, but it hints at the fatal flaw that infects so many CEOs.

Arrogance, from an organizational leadership perspective, is a kind of blinding belief in your own opinions. Under normal circumstances, smart leaders can see when they're being too stubborn, single-minded, and self-righteous. Unfortunately, most leaders today operate under highly stressful circumstances where they don't see how their actions are hurting themselves and their companies. From their perspective, they seem to be operating with the same insight and single-minded vision that helped them rise to their position of prominence. They see resistance as irrational, and their position as infallible.

Are you in danger of becoming a tragic hero? To help answer that question, here's a look at some real leaders we have recently encountered who failed because of arrogance.

Self-Blinding Brilliance

By the age of forty, Linda was a top executive in one of the world's largest global companies. She had the classic pedigree—Ivy League undergraduate, Harvard MBA, a few stellar years at McKinsey, and then a quick climb up the rungs of her current company. If you asked people what Linda was like, their inevitable response was "brilliant." It wasn't just pure intellectual ability. Linda had a knack for solving business problems, for cutting through all the information and verbiage and homing in on just the right answer. She was a leader in the classic mode: assertive, decisive, and highly strategic. It wasn't a question if she'd be a CEO some day; it was just a question of when.

The more position power and influence she gained within the organization, however, the more assertive she became. It reached the point where, according to one of her direct reports, "Linda was no longer able to manage her own arrogance." Her conversations became lectures and her team meetings became a forum for her to belittle ideas that were inconsistent with her point of view. This is not to say that Linda changed in any way. In fact, she became too intensely like herself. She still was coming up with terrific ideas, but they came at a cost. She stopped reading social cues. She didn't get it when her team sat there quietly as she perorated about a new pet project. Slowly but surely, Linda lost trust and respect among her peers. She became so convinced of the rightness of her perspective that she turned others off. People no longer sought her out or wanted to work with her. Not only did she lose some valued direct reports who left to join other functions or teams, she became embroiled in petty feuds with other top executives over direction and resources. Each argument ended with the other executive saying something along the lines of, "You seem to be certain that you're right," and Linda responding, "That's because I am."

She was shocked, therefore, when the CEO called her into his office and told her she was not in line to succeed him and, in fact, would be working for a peer. It wasn't as if she'd never received a signal; the CEO and other senior people had talked to her about the problems her overly confident stances were causing. Linda claimed that she thought they were just coaching suggestions; she assumed her considerable contributions to the company made her invulnerable.

Even after her career ascent was ended, Linda still had trouble believing she had been derailed. She insisted that it was a matter of principle; that she had stood up for what she believed in and the culture of the company wasn't receptive to strong, tough-minded female executives. Though Linda recognized that she was "somewhat intolerant" of views that clashed with her own, she claimed that she was primarily intolerant of "mediocre thinking" and was only seeking to raise the performance standards of her peers.

Linda was justifiably proud of her ideas and accomplishments, but at a certain point, she crossed the line. Her arrogance distorted her view of reality; she failed to see how her actions were affecting others. It wasn't a big distortion, it was a subtle one. When you reach senior leadership levels, however, even small distortions can have a big impact on your career. It was why Linda failed.

Linda, of course, has plenty of company in the arrogance department. The story of Enron's CEO, Jeff Skilling, has been extensively documented by the media. What has not been well documented, however, is how Skilling's pride segued into arrogance. No doubt, Skilling's tremendous confidence in Enron's innovations in trading natural gas and electricity impressed financial analysts. No doubt, his conviction that Enron was a company destined for greatness boosted employee morale and helped attract the best and the brightest. Over time, however, this pride became excessive. It caused the company to display a banner in its lobby proclaiming itself "The World's Leading Company." It prompted Skilling to boast that companies like ExxonMobil would soon become second-tier players and make excessively bold predictions about Enron's share price. He confidently led employee evaluation sessions sarcastically termed "rank and yank" to deal with those who "just didn't get it." If Skilling were not afflicted by arrogance, it seems unlikely that he would have denied mistakes and disavowed wrongdoing even before the U.S. Congress. Arrogance, though, is blinding, and it apparently prevented Skilling from seeing problems that were apparent to everyone else.

Have You Crossed the Line?

Leaders most afflicted by arrogance are the ones most likely to deny its derailing effect on their careers. It helps if you don't think of arrogance as a negative quality that must be eradicated. After all, everyone wants a leader with self-confidence. As you'll discover, the key is learning to step back over the line you crossed (or knowing where the line is before you take that fatal step) from self-confidence to arrogance. The following will give you a sense of the side of the line you're currently on:

You're willing to fight for what you believe in.	You're unwilling to give up a fight no matter what.
You believe that your perspective is the correct one after evaluating other points of view.	You believe that your perspective is the correct one before evaluating others' ideas.
You hold yourself accountable when your strategy or idea doesn't work.	You refuse to take responsibility when your strategy or idea doesn't work.
You adapt your strongly held viewpoint to jibe with new information or developments.	You reinterpret events to fit your point of view.
You possess a powerful ego that allows you to make an impact on others.	You possess a powerful ego that causes you to dominate others.

Remember, arrogance is *a blinding belief in your own opinions,* so you may find yourself rationalizing the results of this exercise. You may insist to yourself that you're on the left side of the line even though you're actually on the right. To make sure you know if this derailer is likely to cause your failure in the future, it's useful to study some classic symptoms of arrogance.

Signs and Symptoms

Arrogance has a tremendous impact on your career and your company, but it can operate in subtle ways during its initial stages. We've known a number of CEOs who recognize they are arrogant but don't recognize that it's severely limiting their capacity to gain the trust of other people. Here are some of the common negative impacts of arrogance:

• *A diminished capacity to learn.* Arrogant leaders reinterpret data to fit their own worldview. Instead of taking in new information and adjusting to it, this type of leader reconfigures the data to fit strongly held views. Thus no learning takes place. Many CEOs today are encountering people, product, and organizational complexities with which they have no experience. Too often, this doesn't stop them from feeling certain they know what to do. Similarly, arrogance discourages other people from giving this type of leader information. They've experienced the contemptuous stare, or the unwillingness to accept an idea contrary to the existing perspective. As a result, people stop trying to provide certain types of information and ideas, knowing they'll be skewered if they do. Arrogance, then, becomes an obstacle to learning. In today's environment, a leader who can't learn and adjust is someone who's bound to fail.

- *An offputting refusal to be accountable.* In other words, such leaders don't take responsibility for their errors. At senior levels, it is easy to blame others: "The organization doesn't get it," "The team didn't execute," or even, "The economy didn't behave." This demoralizes everyone around the leader and often makes bad mistakes worse. Excessive pride prevents people from seeing what they're doing wrong so they end up compounding their mistakes. Even the most brilliant of leaders can act this way. Robert Hogan refers to General Douglas MacArthur's refusing to follow the president's orders during the Korean War and being fired as a result, and MacArthur never was able to admit that he had made a mistake. Many CEO memoirs repeatedly say, "If given a chance, I would do the same thing again!"

- *Resistance to change.* Everyone knows a CEO or other top executive who achieved success doing it "my way" and then refused to depart from an earlier formula for success. These leaders are so absolutely certain that they possess the only right and true map that they resist anything that takes them off their chosen path. Many times they are correct, but more often this position leads to debacle and dismissal. Some of these leaders, however, know they must give the appearance of embracing change. They'll verbally endorse a new strategy and talk about changing with the times. But in their heart of hearts, they're convinced they know what's best and will resist change behind the scenes. This of course sends a confusing message to everyone and makes it difficult if not impossible to implement new policies and programs.

- *An inability to recognize one's limitations.* Arrogant leaders believe that they can do everything well. They are blind to their deficiencies, and this makes them dangerous to themselves and others. To a certain extent, this blindness should be expected. When you've excelled at school, mastered a variety of assignments, and bested your competitors, it's natural that you should feel invincible. The problem, of course, is that this is an illusion. CEOs who believe they can handle every situation and who are willing to make decisions in areas where they have little or no expertise ultimately create tremendous problems for themselves and their organizations.

Pride Goeth Before a Fall: How to Catch Yourself in Time

Arrogance is a treatable disease. Before you fail—or before you cause your group or organization to fail—you can do a number of things to stop yourself short of failure:

- *Determine if you fit the arrogance profile.* CEOs with arrogance follow a remarkably similar path to the top. They achieve great success relatively quickly; they are showered with perks and praise; they passionately believe in their own vision and that they—and only they—are capable to taking the company where it wants to go; they surround themselves with people who share their vision and views. If this sounds like you, reflect upon whether your self-confidence and pride has turned into arrogance.

- *Find the truth-tellers in your organization and ask them to level with you.* This is not the same as telling all your people you have an "open door policy." Overly self-confident, intimidating people frequently have such a policy, but few direct reports take advantage of it because it's very difficult to approach an arrogant leader with anything new or disagreeable. Every company, however, has at least some truth-tellers—people who are almost pathologically direct and honest. Seek them out and ask them how you're perceived. Use the cross-the-line test with them and let them place you on the arrogance continuum.

• *Use setbacks as an opportunity to cross back over the line before a big failure hits.* Sometimes nothing penetrates an arrogant leader's consciousness better than a small failure. At this point, a teachable moment occurs, and it's possible for even the most imperious, brilliant, and visionary CEO to recognize that arrogance will lead to downfall. As with all the derailers, arrogance-generated failure is an opportunity as well as a setback. Many times, derailers destroy careers because we're unwilling to acknowledge the trait that is making us less effective than we should be. We're so convinced that a given trait is "who we are" and why we're successful that we're reluctant to see the trait's dark side. Failure, though, gives us pause. It is especially useful for arrogant leaders who rarely stop and consider their vulnerabilities and flaws. This is the time to think long and hard about whether your excessive pride may have contributed to the setback. This is the time to ask the truth-tellers in your organization for brutally honest feedback. If you accumulate enough evidence that your arrogance was the culprit, you may be motivated to change.

Different Forms, Same Results

As you contemplate your arrogance, be aware that it manifests itself in different ways. The classic way is the visibly arrogant, insistently right leader who rules an organization as if born to the throne. It's also possible, however, for arrogance to catalyze failure in a less obvious manner; arrogance can be internalized, resulting in behaviors that look different but still reflect the same trait. Here's a look at these two extremes of arrogance, starting with the classic model.

Al Dunlap, formerly CEO of Sunbeam and Scott Paper, features in perhaps the best-known story of CEO arrogance. Dunlap's radical actions after becoming CEO of Sunbeam, undertaken in the name of "increasing shareholder value," were applauded at the time: reducing labor costs, closing factories, and controlling expenses. His disregard for the impact of his decisions on people earned him the nickname "Chainsaw Al." What is less well known is that while undertaking these actions, Dunlap also gave himself large pay increases, first-class air fares, and a free Mercedes car. Although the Sunbeam headquarters was in Florida, Dunlap demanded the right to stay at the Four Seasons Hotel when he visited his dentist in Pennsylvania, among other executive perquisites he required to help him manage the stresses and demands of his job.

Dunlap's style has since been discredited, and he endured and settled shareholder lawsuits about his role as CEO. But his case is illustrative, and not entirely different from that of many leaders who come to identify with their appointed role, believing in not only their infallibility but also their entitlement. Dennis Kozlowski, John Rigas, Samuel Waskal, and Joseph Nacchio are examples of CEOs whose excessive belief in their own self-worth, at least as evidenced by their pay packages and decision-making processes, blinded them to the real interests of their shareholders.

Contrast this classic example of arrogance with another, different version we've encountered. Matt was the division president of a very large corporation. No one would accuse him of being closed-minded or surrounding himself with yes-men. He had a real open door policy, and people used it. Matt, however, committed the sin of arrogance, albeit in a more subtle manner than Dunlap. Matt was a process guy; he firmly believed that process excellence was the answer to everything. It was his religion, and it had served him well throughout his career. As a result, he tried to force process into his company's market and sales-driven culture. When people resisted his efforts, he ignored their resistance and kept pushing. His almost obsessive certainty that process excellence would solve everything ultimately alienated everyone, including the company's CEO. We worked closely with the CEO, and we warned Matt clearly that his arrogance was going to get him fired. Unfortunately, his blinding confidence in his own views made our feedback irrelevant. Despite the warning, he persisted, convinced that his company's weaknesses must yield to his process focus and that his crusade would vindicate him by delivering better results. Matt was eventually fired—not because his process ideas were bad or even wrong for this company, but because he couldn't adapt his ideas to the company's culture and core strengths.

Arrogance, therefore, can be highly visible and more subtle. In either case, it can lead to the downfall of careers and companies.

CHAPTER TWO

Melodrama

You Always Grab the Center of Attention

I t's difficult to be a successful CEO without some presence. Today, many organizations expect their leaders to have charisma and even showmanship. In many cases the personality of the CEO blends with the brand of the company—creating a dynamic and persuasive image. In an era where image matters, especially with financial analysts, customers, and employees, it is important for the chief executive to hold an audience.

At times, you probably have found it necessary to be overly dramatic to make a point. Like a good actor, you raised your voice in a meeting to communicate to direct reports the seriousness of a situation. Or you may have resorted to hyperbole during an important presentation to make an impression.

Melodrama means exaggerated emotion or action. In theater, the term suggests an over-the-top performance or plot that detracts from the play's message. In organizations, melodrama is a derailer because it detracts from other people's performances and impairs a leader's ability to see what's going on. Let's look at how a charismatic and successful leader crosses the line into melodrama.

Sparks Fly When Bob Walks in the Room— Which Is Why His Company Went Down in Flames

As the CEO of a mid-sized ad agency, Bob was known throughout the business as a great presenter. Bob rose to head the agency, in fact, because of his almost legendary ability to mesmerize clients during new business presentations. Handsome, athletic, and tall, Bob commanded the stage not only because he looked the part and was a great presenter but because he was very smart about advertising and his clients' industries. Clients not only liked how he said things, they liked what he said. On more than one occasion, Bob had come up with advertising strategies that resulted in breakthrough campaigns that won awards and spurred significant sales increases.

Bob's agency, like most ad agencies, was hit hard by the recent advertising downturn. Clients cut ad budgets and new business was difficult to come by. One of the ways Bob responded was with motivating speeches to the troops. He'd walk in unannounced to a meeting and tell them how the new business pitch they were working on was the single most important pitch in the agency's history—Bob would say this about most of the new business pitches. Bob also dominated strategy meetings. Bob loved the spotlight. But his manner and tone intimidated others and inhibited them from making suggestions. In meetings, Bob would proclaim the agency was about to turn the corner and was going to surprise everyone with a terrific quarter. At first, these inspirational messages achieved Bob's goal of boosting morale— he was tremendously convincing, and people believed in him. After a while, however, people took the messages as routine and more than one person noted that they'd "seen Bob's act one too many times."

When a key account defected, Bob lost credibility. Then a number of talented account and creative people left the agency, feeling that he was ignoring their ideas. Eventually, the agency's owners—the agency had been acquired by a larger agency a few years before Bob had been named CEO—ordered a massive downsizing and fired him.

Two Showboats with Nothing to Show

Vivendi Universal's Jean-Marie Messier and Qwest Communications' Joseph P. Nacchio enjoyed great success in large part because of their dramatic, attention-getting style. Messier displayed great chutzpah—or perhaps we should say savoir faire—as he turned a French waste management company into the world's second-largest media conglomerate. He relentlessly acquired company after company and was dubbed by the French press the "master of the universe." But the more he bought, the more intense the financial pressure as debt mounted. Vivendi's stock dropped by 70 percent and concerns about cash flow developed. Ultimately, Messier resigned and Vivendi Universal is in the process of being broken up and sold off.

It seems fair to conclude that Messier got carried away. He so thoroughly embraced his role as a globe-trotting CEO and industry-redefining leader that he said and did things that came back to haunt him. He bought many companies quickly, a quintessential melodramatic (and megalomaniacal) strategy to display a leader's brilliance to the world. He offended Frenchmen with his move to New York and statements that some of his countrymen interpreted as anti-French. It's telling that in his farewell statement to the company, he explained that he was leaving in order to "save" the company and that "It is for you that I wanted to fight right to the end." His sense of drama may well have distorted his sense of reality. He played the imperial CEO to the end, but he might have been better served if he had taken on a quieter role and thought before he acted.

In 2002, Nacchio of Qwest saw his company's stock price and credit rating plummet and faced SEC questioning about its accounting methods. He resigned in the middle of the year— some reports say that his board pressured him to resign. It was not that long since he had been triumphant, having orchestrated Qwest's $58 billion acquisition of U.S. West. It was a hostile takeover, and during the negotiations Nacchio made a number of statements to the press painting U.S. West as a bureaucratic mess and describing its executives in colorfully negative terms. A *Forbes* article at the time describes how after the acquisition, he told U.S. West Wireless head Peter Mannetti that he had thirty minutes to change the U.S. West sign on his office building to Qwest if he wanted to keep his job.

Certainly Nacchio was under tremendous pressure after making the acquisition of U.S. West—layoffs and other tough measures had to be taken—and it seems likely that this pressure may have fueled some of his more outrageous statements. Instead of trying to mend fences as is customary after a hostile acquisition, Nacchio was as controversial and outspoken as he was before. Like Messier's, this style made enemies, raised unrealistic expectations, and pushed him past the point of no return. As Kaufman Brothers communications services analyst Vik Grover said of Nacchio at the time, "He had lost credibility with Wall Street, he lost credibility with customers and lost credibility with employees."

Many CEOs feel compelled to live "larger than life"—with waiting limousines, private jets, several homes, and even expensive shower curtains. These role artifacts consume attention and signal importance—but also create a dangerous downside for a leader—they induce separation from others and make open, honest dialogue and problem solving difficult, if not impossible.

Have You Crossed the Line?

Messier, Nacchio, and Bob failed because their theatrical, attention-getting personas were distorted under stress. Their strengths as leaders turned into derailers as financial pressures intensified. As you become familiar with the other derailers, you'll find that stress often turns leadership strengths into negative, failure-inducing traits. In Bob's case, his amazing capacity to make presentations to outsiders turned into an obsessive theatricality inside the agency. He transformed meetings into chamber dramas, and everyone became tired of his style—especially when he failed to achieve the results he promised. He neglected people's need for authenticity and honest answers, failing to draw on their strengths to improve the business. Though Bob had substance, he overrelied on style to deal with difficult issues. In Messier's and Nacchio's cases, the CEOs themselves became the issue, rather than the plans and strategies their companies were pursuing.

Just as you can unknowingly cross the line from pride to arrogance, you can make a similar journey from impressive impact to melodrama. To help you be aware whether you've crossed the line, consider the following and see which side of the line you're on:

| You command attention when you speak. | You dominate meetings by speaking constantly. |

You use charisma to involve and motivate people.	You use attention-getting style to create unquestioning compliance.
Your showmanship helps attract outside attention from media, analysts, and prospective recruits.	Your highly theatrical style creates the impression that your style of leadership is the issue for discussion.
You know exactly when to be charming or deliver an eloquent talk to achieve a key goal.	You are consistently flamboyant rather than strategically dramatic.
You can turn off the style and listen and learn from others.	You're always "on" and rarely reflect on what you're trying to achieve.

As you attempt to determine which side of the line you're on, be aware that leaders who cross the line are those who place the act above the action. In other words, they become caught up in seeking attention and fail to enlarge the circle of leadership to include others whose views are equally important to the success of the company. If you find yourself acting like the star rather than the director of the production, the odds are you've crossed over to the dark side.

Signs and Symptoms

While not all melodramatic leaders act alike, most exhibit obvious behaviors that suggest they're on the path to failure. Keep the following signs and symptoms in mind as you assess your capacity for melodrama:

• *Lack of focus.* While melodramatic leaders can be engaging, outgoing, and interpersonally skillful, they can lose sight of what's important. The melodramatic leader will often say whatever comes to mind in order to impress, motivate, or attract attention. The problem, of course, is that the resulting comments may not be altogether coherent or congruent so the listeners have trouble "connecting the dots." People get confused about what the priorities are, resulting in wasted energy as they scatter in different directions.

• *A failure to develop people.* It's not that melodramatic leaders purposefully set out to stifle others. It's simply the force of their personality that gets in their way. Melodramatic executives distract attention from others and focus attention on themselves. People feel that their opinions aren't wanted or needed. In some instances, they're intimidated by the melodramatic tone and presentation of this type of leader. Quieter, less assertive direct reports are especially disadvantaged when they have melodramatic bosses; they don't feel the impetus to take risks, gain air time in meetings, or develop as leaders themselves. Melodramatic CEOs often lead teams populated with conservative, compliant direct reports who function well behind the scenes but can't aspire to the spotlight.

• *Showboating teams.* In some cases, melodramatic leaders take the opposite tack and surround themselves with people who are prone to copy the melodramatic boss's style. It can be an attractive style, and it seems to get you noticed, so why not replicate it? If you've ever been in a meeting with a group of melodramatic executives, however, you know the downside of this style. Everyone is talking at once, attempting to out-argue and out-act the others. Little gets accomplished, but all the pontificating makes it feel like a lot is being done. We've witnessed Executive Committees that resemble frat parties—each member a "character in his own right" and determined to prove it.

- *Elevated expectations.* Though we've listed this last, it's a particularly pernicious repercussion. Melodramatic leaders often start out with a bang. Typically, they possess superior social skills, make great first impressions, and are promoted swiftly. They develop a following, a cadre of acolytes who believe their man or woman is headed toward the top. At some point, though, their expectations are dashed because they fail to follow through on commitments. They may talk a good game about the company successfully beating a competitor, or how they're going to acquire and expand their base, or how next year looks like a record year that will bring big bonuses, but they don't deliver on their promises and projections. People lose confidence in these leaders and feel like they've been misled.

Dialing Down the Volume

Like many successful leaders, Martin was promoted in part because of his powerful presence. An ex-military man from an Eastern establishment family, Martin had gone to West Point and been the quarterback of his high school and college lacrosse teams. Solidly built and square-jawed, and with a deep, booming voice, Martin was someone who seemed born to command. He enjoyed a quick ascent at a global consumer products company and then a headhunter recruited him for a country manager position at an even larger corporation. Eventually, the CEO of his new company thought Martin was one of three internal candidates to be considered as part of the succession process—he was planning to retire within three years—but he was concerned about Martin's tendency to fall back on "bluster and blarney" under certain circumstances. The CEO had observed that when Martin faced a difficult situation that was either outside of his experience or lacking a clear-cut answer, he relied on his rhetorical skills. Rather than say "I don't know," engage in additional research, or encourage his team to come up with better ideas, Martin would give performances. He'd exaggerate problems, using colorful hyperbole to describe a difficult situation and impressing listeners with his fascinating analysis. Or he'd tell great stories that were highly entertaining and took people's minds off the problem. People would walk away from an encounter with Martin thinking he was brilliant and mesmerizing.

Unfortunately, he was also failing as a leader. Though he'd been told in the past by coaches and bosses to tone down his style and focus on the business issues more directly and quickly, he never really made much effort to change. Martin was convinced that people were jealous of his speaking skills and that his ability to persuade others was part of his effectiveness. It was only when a coach sat down with Martin and provided clear feedback from others and a list of situations where Martin had failed to deliver in the eyes of others that the lesson sunk in. The coach shared feedback and painful quotations from Martin's direct reports and bosses that clearly communicated times when Martin's showmanship did not address a problem—and in some cases exacerbated it. The accumulated weight of all that feedback had an impact. Finally, Martin was able to acknowledge that his melodramatic tendencies could be a derailer and he needed to do something about it. He began by consistently thinking before speaking, and consciously giving others opportunities to interrupt, ask questions, and challenge. He didn't change his personality but he adapted his style—and he remains on the list as possible successors to the CEO.

If you're a melodramatic leader, you need to pay attention to feedback about your impact on others. The good news is that this particular derailer is highly responsive to feedback. Unlike many of the other derailers, this one is relatively easy to deal with. To avoid failure from melodrama, you usually don't have to make major changes in how you lead and manage. Instead, it's more a matter of reducing the volume. Simply acknowledging and becoming more aware of these derailing behaviors can be all that's needed. Therefore, listen for feedback about your impact as Martin did. Here are some other techniques we've found to be effective with melodramatic leaders:

• *Get someone to videotape you in action.* Melodramatic behavior—and its impact—is highly visible. Having someone tape you in action can be an eye-opening experience, especially if they capture you in team meetings or addressing other groups when your melodramatic behavior is evident. As you view the videotape, ask yourself the following questions:

Am I dominating discussions to the point that no one is volunteering fresh information or ideas? Do people seem hesitant to do anything more than add to my points or agree with me?

Is my audience really with me? Or are their eyes glazed? Does it seem as if I have sucked all the energy and enthusiasm from the room with my animated style?

Do I use my dynamism and eloquence selectively or is it a uniform style? Do I use it to deal effectively with a specific problem or issue or does it seem to be a random style?

• *Identify the circumstances that cause you to cross the line into melodrama.* As you become more aware of your melodramatic behavior, you'll be able to track the catalysts of this reflex. Do you resort to being a domineering presence when under stress? Do you do so when trying to motivate direct reports? Are there certain types of meetings or people who bring out the theatrical side of your personality? Noting when you're more likely to act up or act out allows you to be aware of your specific melodramatic triggers. Being aware of these triggers gives you a way to monitor your behaviors in circumstances where you're vulnerable.

• *Make time to reflect and listen.* Melodramatic leaders generally aren't very comfortable with extended periods of quiet and contemplation. Nor are they willing to consistently solicit other people's input and attempt to understand their needs. If you make a conscious effort to reflect and listen, you'll naturally tone down your melodramatic instincts. Reflection will help you realize that always wanting to be the center of attention has its downside. If you take a moment to think about it, you'll understand that your strength as a speaker and motivator is also a weakness if it doesn't allow other people to contribute. Similarly, if you work hard at listening to what your people need from you and from the company (and this means more than perfunctory conversations where your mind is elsewhere or where you dominate the discussion), you'll find opportunities to let others take the spotlight.

Melodrama has become an especially powerful derailer as companies move away from command-and-control personalities and require leaders to be better listeners and observers. Years ago, before matrix structures and complex business interdependencies were commonplace, melodramatic behavior was less risky. Today, however, it can deprive a leader of the capacity to develop other leaders and involve a wider range of people in decision making and innovation. The task of following a melodramatic CEO in the job is a difficult one, made more so by the fact that many of these successors have had to labor far outside the limelight before assuming it. The dramatic leader is still a valuable commodity in a media-driven business environment, but this value is diminished when the showmanship isn't used wisely and selectively.

CHAPTER THREE

Volatility

Your Mood Shifts Are Sudden and Unpredictable

Given the complex challenges that confront leaders today, it is no wonder that CEOs might experience tremendous mood swings. In today's volatile environment, it's easy to go from wild optimism to frustration. Larry Ellison, Harvey Weinstein, and Steve Jobs are just three leaders whose volatile personalities are legendary; one day they're erupting in anger and the next they're exuding encouragement and empathy. An argument can be made that volatility is a prerequisite for being CEO. Volatile leaders vibrate with energy that can be contagious for an organization. In their positive, energized period, they command attention and respect, motivating and inspiring those around them in ways that others can't. Their negative, bad-tempered phase is excused as a natural reaction to the job's frustrations or as the price that has to be paid for the expenditure of all that energy.

CEOs like Ellison, Weinstein, and Jobs, though, aren't slaves of their volatile nature but masters of it. Most of the time, they use their sudden enthusiasms and excitement purposefully; they want to draw attention to an issue or demonstrate their support for a project or to raise a red flag so no one misses it.

For some CEOs and other executives, volatility turns into a derailer. In their youth, it may well have helped get them noticed, facilitating their career ascent. When they get to the CEO's office, however, their volatility carries greater risk. It makes them seem unpredictable. Though it would be hyperbole to claim that volatile leaders are Jeckyll-and-Hydes or bipolar personalities, they can swing from one mood to another in a way that makes them very hard to predict. Though these leaders throw off great energy, they ironically can also drain it away as people attempt to adjust to their moods.

If you're vulnerable to this derailer, then you'll probably identify with the following true examples of highly talented people who were brought down by their volatile traits.

Who's Going to Show Up Today?

Here are two stories of mood-swinging leaders. . . .

Andrew was CEO of a fast-growing, highly successful global software business. He was an experienced leader who had been CEO and COO of several large technology companies and influenced most aspects of his latest company because of his lengthy résumé and strong presence. Andrew didn't fit the classic volatile profile. Introverted and somewhat inarticulate, he'd attend two-day strategy meetings and say very little over the course of these two days. He might ask some great questions, but he'd give his people plenty of opportunities to talk and joke. At some point, usually during the later stages of these two-day meetings, however, Andrew would start to get that "look." Everyone who had worked with him for a while would know which issues would incite the rumblings. He'd start fidgeting in his chair and his eyes would go dark and steely. Then all of a sudden he'd jump out of his chair, slamming his hand on the table, waving his arms in the air, and shouting. Because of his position and the unpredictability of his explosion, the effect was intimidating. People literally cowered as Andrew railed, avoiding eye contact in case they would incur his wrath.

Veterans of these meetings became aware of the issues that triggered Andrew's outbursts—usually implementation roadblocks, country strategies not aligned with corporate strategy, or surprise moves by the competition that were not anticipated through competitive analysis—and tried to avoid bringing them up. This was bad for the strategic planning process—plans were flawed because issues that needed to be addressed were unofficially off-limits. Despite their effort to avoid tough issues, though, Andrew would still find something that would set him off.

A COO was recruited to help the business expand, and a great deal of time and effort went into getting the best person possible. The new COO, Greg, was terrific, and Andrew fully endorsed the hire. Greg was a sensitive, compassionate, people-oriented leader with strong personal values about how people should be treated. The first few times Andrew blew up in a meeting, Greg was stunned. He had not witnessed this type of behavior in any of his previous companies, and he told everyone, "I'm not going to put up with this." Andrew, of course, didn't see the problem and made no effort to manage his volatility. When informed of Greg's reactions, he dismissed his concerns as "not ready for prime time." Greg complained about Andrew to everyone, including the Board, and created an open rift at the top. He eventually departed, which was a big blow to the company from which it still hasn't recovered.

Unlike Andrew, Claire was usually articulate and vivacious. As a top HR executive in one of the country's largest companies, Claire was terrific at attracting talent and generating excitement about projects among her people. She was warm and effusive in her compliments and could make her direct reports feel terrific. Smart and analytical, Claire was a gifted executive who could reconceptualize HR and brought a lot of value to the company. Yet there were days when she was neither warm nor complimentary. On her bad days, little things would get to her, and she'd criticize almost anyone on any issue who came within her range. Not only would she go after direct reports, she would be hostile toward her peers, accusing them of undermining HR.

As a result, Claire created disequilibrium. She wasn't able to sustain commitment among her direct reports, despite the fact that many of them had joined the company because of her. One day Claire might be incredibly generous, and provide great coaching and support, and the next day she might criticize the same person as a blundering incompetent. Her colleagues felt drained after interactions with Claire on her bad days, and soon Claire was considered "high-maintenance." This reputation prevented her from being effective, and her career essentially stalled.

At this point, you may be thinking that these are extreme cases, and you're not like Andrew or Claire. You're not explosive. If you become angry, you do so in a controlled, constructive way. Sometimes, however, volatility doesn't manifest itself in an obvious form—shifts in mood can be far subtler. You may keep your behavior on a relatively even keel, but inside you're experiencing dramatic mood swings. When you're "up," you're fine, but when you experience a dark mood, you lose your enthusiasm; you may move through meetings and conversations unemotionally, enervated or uncertain. While your behavior may not seem extreme to others, your mood changes your perspective enough to have an impact on your perception and hence on your performance. Your controlled expression hides your lethargy and your unwillingness to put much time or effort into achieving a goal. One day you can be highly optimistic about a project and talk eloquently and convincingly about its upside; the next day you're all doom and gloom and can't see how it will ever get off the ground. You have trouble finding middle ground. Volatility can create failure even when its effects are largely internal.

Have You Crossed the Line?

Volatile leaders don't fail because they fly off the handle now and then. Because of the difficulty of getting things done through others and the uncertainty and challenges any business environment presents, CEOs and senior leaders are bound to experience highs and lows. The line is crossed, though, when they experience them frequently, intensely, and unconsciously. Are you likely to fail because of your volatility? See if you've crossed the line:

You lose your temper because of major screw-ups or other significant problems.	You explode over minor mistakes or for reasons you can't articulate.
Feedback tells you that your people know what they can expect from you.	Feedback tells you that your people don't know who's going to show up from one day to the next.
You generally act one way most of the time.	You move back and forth between optimistic and pessimistic stances.

You consistently generate energy and enthusiasm through your words and deeds.	You create energy and enthusiasm one day and intimidate others the next through your words and actions.
You change the way you act in order to achieve a specific effect.	You feel like events or your moods create changes in how you normally act.

Signs and Symptoms

Volatile leaders often don't see the impact their volatility is having on their careers. They may be aware of their mood swings, and they may even realize others find them off-putting, but they don't grasp just how seriously this trait can undermine effectiveness. Moreover, volatility combined with organizational or position power can sometimes equal abuse, with serious consequences.

For this reason, pay careful attention to the following red flags that signal volatility could be a major problem for you:

• *People hold back in their interactions with you.* Have you noticed that your direct reports aren't forthcoming? Do they find it difficult to deliver bad news about failures, missed commitments, or unexpected events, or do they consistently avoid certain topics? Fear of your unpredictable outbursts may be cutting off your information flow. If this is the case, you're likely to make decisions in the dark—or at least in poor light. If you can identify certain topics that everyone avoids when you're around, your volatile nature may be to blame. Invariably, you're going to make bad decisions with serious consequences because of incomplete information.

• *There's a lot of mood management going on around you.* The classic case of mood management is when people consult your secretary for a "weather report" before entering your office and adjust their behavior accordingly. Your direct reports try to read you; they're tentative when they first approach, attempting to figure out if you're in the right mood to broach a touchy subject. People don't seem to be behaving naturally; your unpredictability causes them to say and do things that they normally wouldn't say or do or to avoid things that would be routine on better days. Because they invest their energy in managing your moods, they monitor their own behavior, the conversation is controlled, and you can sense that they're not connecting.

• *You feel like people are becoming increasingly distant.* More specifically, your phone calls are returned with well-rehearsed answers, direct reports and colleagues are making an effort to stay out of your way, relatively few people are seeking your input, even as CEO. You're not invited to share your point of view on an issue and must inject it. What all this could signify is that people don't want to deal with the emotional baggage of a volatile leader. If they can't figure out when you're going to explode or go into a pessimistic funk, they find it wiser to keep their distance and maintain control.

Although the most obvious symptom of volatility to others is a frequent and dramatic mood swing, it probably won't be the most obvious symptom to you. It's great if you can become aware that you're rocketing between positive and negative moods, but you may have difficulty seeing these swings for what they are, especially if you're a CEO or other top executive. What looks like volatility to others feels to you like a normal reaction to the stress of leadership. Therefore, watch for the previously noted symptoms to identify whether this derailer will cause you to fail. Many volatile leaders complain they can't control their emotional outbursts—that they come from out of the blue and can't be anticipated. We have seen that with some work and perseverance volatile leaders can learn to monitor the warning signs and manage the expression of their mood swings.

How to Keep Volatility from Exploding in Your Face

A little bit of awareness and self-regulation can keep volatility at bay. Here are two things you can do in this regard:

• *Empower a trusted adviser to give you a volatility alert.* Ideally, you know someone you've worked with for years and who is willing and able to tell you when you're bouncing from highs to lows or when you're stuck in a "the end is near" mindset. In most cases, though, you need to establish an implicit contract before even a close associate will feel empowered to give you honest feedback without worrying about repercussions. (Killing the messenger is a well-established tradition in such situations, so even close friends may be wary of you—and rightly so.) If you find that there's no one in your organization to fill this role, you may need an outside coach who can speak to you honestly and intervene when you're getting yourself in trouble. It's not unusual for CEOs to employ such a coach to speak about issues employees won't or can't. With one of our clients, we watched for signs of her volatility emerging and suggested she "settle down" whenever it threatened to spin out of control. She was much more willing to settle down when we demonstrated how her people saw her when she lost it; how they just saw this huge outpouring of emotion and didn't see her receptivity and openness, traits she prized.

• *Learn to take a step back . . . or a step forward.* Reflection can cool you down before you go into a rage. Forcing yourself to see possibilities and opportunities can prevent you from sinking into a doom-and-gloom shell. Admittedly, these aren't easy things for a CEO to do, especially in the heat of battle. A general in Vietnam gave the following advice to his platoon leaders to use during battles, and we've found that this advice also serves volatile leaders well:

Ask what's happening, what's not happening, and how can I influence the action.

Translated, this means you should consciously take a step away from your interpersonal reaction to people and events. Before doing anything, contemplate for a moment what it is you really want to achieve by your words and deeds. Check in with your own intentions and see how well your intentions line up with your potential impact if you give free rein to your emotions. The gap between intention and impact is where most leadership careers derail.

Volatility only causes failure when the tremendous energy thrown off by a leader is misused. Channeling this energy productively—and refusing to allow its expenditure to drain you—should be your focus.

Great Leaders Are Not Always Great Managers

Your volatile nature may create great energy in the company and fuel your vision. You may be able to out-work and out-think everyone else when you get rolling, and you're the best possible spokesperson for the vision. Your energy is contagious, and everyone from the media to financial analysts may buy in to your vision. Others may describe you as a heroic, idea-generating, charismatic leader.

But these same leadership qualities can have a negative impact on your management style. We'd like to share with you the story of a CEO who embodies this dilemma. It's a bit different from some of our other stories of CEO failure, in that this man recognized how the derailer was affecting him and made a change before it caused serious problems for his organization.

Halsey Minor was the co-founder of online media company CNet. In a very short time, he built the company into an Internet powerhouse with a thousand employees and revenue of $38 million. Then he resigned, remaining as chairman of the company but turning over the CEO position to his co-founder. Though he resigned ostensibly because he wanted to pursue other Internet investments, he may well have realized that his management style wasn't particularly conducive to running an established company. For one thing, during the first five years of the company's existence, he'd run the company without a formal employee evaluation program or a budgeting system.

More disturbing, however, were the reports that he swung between giving his people excessive praise to excoriating them in e-mail blasts. In one article about Minor, a CNet executive was quoted as saying, "It's sort of a company joke. How many 'Flame-mails' did you get from Halsey at 6 A.M.?"

Minor's seeming recognition that he performed better in business-creation situations rather than business-management ones probably saved him and his organization a lot of money. Unfortunately, not all leaders are as perceptive about their de-railers.

CHAPTER FOUR

Excessive Caution

The Next Decision You Make May Be Your First

It's not surprising that some CEOs are overly cautious. What's surprising is that so few of them are this way. More now than ever before, CEOs are under scrutiny, and their actions and words are examined for clues to a company's future (and its stock price). They must keep one eye on newly aggressive boards and the other on newly aggressive regulatory bodies. All this while watching out for new pension funding requirements, new competitive threats, new technologies, new accounting requirements, new medical costs, new bond ratings, new cash flow requirements, new litigation, and all the other factors that can threaten their success.

Therefore, if being overly cautious is your derailer, the current environment makes you highly vulnerable to it. You may find yourself overanalyzing important decisions in the face of increased anxiety and significant stress. Your fear of making the wrong decision causes you to procrastinate. Instead of making a choice, you delve deeper into the data. You want one more study, one more task force. Pretty soon, the problem has spiraled out of control or the opportunity has been missed, and the very failure you sought to avoid is brought about by indecision.

Overly cautious, however, isn't the phrase that you'd use to describe this behavior. You would characterize yourself as *prudent* or *thorough,* and to a certain extent, this characterization would be accurate. Throughout your career, your strength has been analyzing situations astutely and then moving forward only after you've covered all the bases. You make very few mistakes, and this has helped you succeed. Problems occur, though, when you become intensely and consistently cautious and can't pull the trigger when it needs to be pulled. You may tell yourself you just need one more round of analysis before you make your decision, but the reality is that no amount of analysis will be sufficient.

Today, CEOs who are overly cautious frequently fail. There's just too much data to analyze. Lloyd Ward at Maytag is a CEO whose caution led directly or indirectly to failure. He was described as failing to act decisively at important moments. In certain situations, leaders need to act without possessing all the data they would like. "He who hesitates is lost" is one adage the overly cautious CEO should heed. Combining instinct and experience to seize the moment is something just about every CEO needs to do. Here are some examples of leaders who may have intellectually recognized the importance of seizing the moment, but whose unconscious impulse toward caution prevented them from doing so.

Knowledge Is Not Always Power

Frank, an engineer by training, was CEO of a Fortune 100 company. Over the years, he had demonstrated great savvy regarding technological issues, and he had made very wise decisions about investing in new technology based on careful, highly perceptive analysis. When Frank became CEO, though, his decision-making process was the same as when he was head of the company's engineering function. Whenever his people presented him with a proposal or project, he demanded endless studies, mind-numbing backup data, and countless tests. After a while, everyone became accustomed to his modus operandi and responded accordingly.

Instead of focusing the organization on external trends and developments, Frank inadvertently focused it on internal matters. People concentrated on feeding Frank's insatiable appetite for data. Rather than investing their time in productive work, they spent much of their time and energy in trying to anticipate and satisfy his requests.

In the long run, this misspent time and energy crippled the company. While competitors moved forward, launching innovative new products and services, buying, selling, and diversifying, Frank's company lagged behind. It wasn't that the competitors' launches were uniformly successful, it was that Frank's company, as the leader in the industry, became known as a conservative, risk-averse organization. The metamorphosis was gradual, accompanied by quarterly reports of less-than-stellar revenue growth and earnings. As a result, the most talented techies gravitated toward faster-growth companies. Some key executives who were frustrated with Frank's indecisiveness left to assume top positions in competing organizations. After a number of years, his company dropped from its leadership position and Frank was retired out of the company. After his departure, the company was merged with another and no longer exists.

Former President Jimmy Carter is a great nonbusiness example of an overly cautious leader. In a way, though, he epitomized the CEOs of an earlier era. Data-driven, analytical, and focused on all the things that might go wrong, Carter was ineffectual in many policy areas. Our CDR International partner, Steven Rhinesmith, has compared Carter's decision-making style to that of President Ronald Reagan. Carter would come to a decision only after reading numerous reports, some of which would argue radically different points of view. For example, he might receive reports from the Defense Department and the State Department that took opposing positions, but each report was eloquent and persuasive. He often vacillated between positions because he was unable to analyze his way to a solution. As a result, he was often described as indecisive. Reagan, on the other hand, made decisions based on a clear-cut system of beliefs and values such as smaller government, stronger defense, and lower taxes. Using these beliefs as a guide, Reagan made faster, bolder decisions than Carter, and is generally considered to have been a more effective leader.

Have You Crossed the Line?

In one sense, crossing the line means going from being prudent to being overly cautious. Any context, however, can create a razor-thin line. In certain circumstances and in certain cultures, being prudent means acting in ways that could be described as overly cautious. If many of today's troubled or bankrupt companies had been overly cautious about their financial reporting, they would be counting cash rather than borrowing it. There are times when it's suicidal to be anything but cautious.

In our experience, leaders fail when they are routinely and philosophically cautious rather than situationally prudent. The following exercise will help you determine on which side of the line you fall:

You analyze a situation before you make a decision.	You require second and third opinions before making any decision.

You look at worst-case scenarios before moving forward.	You obsess about what might go wrong and eventually get stuck.
You go slow before deciding because the wrong decision can have serious consequences.	You go slow before deciding because you believe every decision can have serious consequences.
You turn down requests for projects and resources when you have hard evidence that flaws exist.	You don't give people the go-ahead because of your fears that a proposed project is flawed.

Signs and Symptoms

Overly cautious leaders give off clear signals that they're headed toward failure. The most obvious one, of course, is the inability to make a big decision when necessary. You've probably worked with someone who constantly sits on every decision. Clearly, this type of person is bound to fail because a leader has to take some kind of action. But there are more subtle signs you should pay heed to, including

• *Unwillingness to fire anyone.* To the overly cautious executive, any significant action entails major risk, and that's cause enough to shy away from action. This type of leader may come up with all sorts of excuses for not letting someone go—he's been with the company for years, her pluses outweigh her minuses, he has too much potential—but it's obvious to everyone this employee is a bad fit. The real reason the overly cautious leader won't fire anyone is the conviction that it will lead to a terrible consequence—poor morale, high turnover, and so on. Variations on the failure-to-act theme include unwillingness to enter a new market, to form an alliance, to make an acquisition, or launch a product without extensive and excessive market testing. All these actions entail risk, and the overly cautious leader wants nothing to do with risk, especially when things aren't going well. Failure results because a certain amount of action—and risk—is necessary for forward movement. If you never fire anyone, you will be stuck with at least some underperforming people, and the longer you're in the job, the more underperformers you'll be saddled with. The inability to act decisively on underperforming but loyal subordinates is a key predictor of CEO failure.

- *Churn instead of movement.* The overly cautious leader gives the illusion of doing something by doing little things that don't entail much risk—making a show of forming committees and setting timetables, of doing elaborate white papers and restructuring departments. But in the end, nothing much is accomplished. People spend inordinate amounts of time on what they think is a major project only to be frustrated when they learn that it was never implemented. Failure flows from frustration, especially when rising expectations are crushed by the reality of an overly cautious CEO.

- *Absence of strong opinions or engagement in debate.* Highly cautious leaders prefer to remain on the sidelines during discussions, rarely offering their own point of view. This may seem a strange behavior for a CEO, but it's more common than you might expect. Such CEOs see themselves as being watchfully wise, weighing all sides of the issue before making a decision, but their silence is indicative of a fear of rejection. They don't want to take a stand for fear of being criticized or contradicted, or of having to engage in contentious debate. Being conflict averse, they prefer to insulate themselves behind an air of neutrality. The problem, of course, is that this neutral position creates a lack of direction and forward movement. Failure comes because the company is drifting rather than moving toward an objective.

What's the Worst That Can Happen: Remaining Cautious to the Point of Indecisiveness

Overly cautious leaders tend to fail slowly rather than quickly. Overwhelmed by their fear of failure from a single mistake, they get failure in phases. Missed opportunities and unresolved problems accumulate over time until it's too late for action. The good news is that this derailer gives you plenty of time to act before it's too late. Here are some things we've found to be effective for leaders in this position:

• *Prioritize.* It seems simple, but if you're an overly cautious leader, this is a tough thing to do. You need to make a list of all the issues you're facing and prioritize the one or two key matters you have to make decisions about. Circle these key items, set limits on your data gathering, and give yourself a decision date and hold yourself to it. Keep reminding yourself that even if you make a bad decision, you may be less likely to fail than if you make no decision at all.

• *Do something different.* At the risk of making broad psychological assumptions, we would suggest that people who are overly cautious are wary of the unfamiliar. They don't decide or assert themselves because it would lead them into unknown territory. One antidote to this wariness is making a concerted effort to do something you've never done before. If you've never walked around the factory floor, try walking around. If you've never engaged in debate in a meeting, do so. You might even want to carry this action over to your personal life. Go sailing, drive to work by a different route, or do something unfamiliar—regularly. Refuse to be a prisoner of your experience. When you realize that nothing horrible happens when you try something new, you're less likely to be stuck in your cautious mode.

• *Focus on past successes.* What keeps some leaders from being more decisive is an irrational fear of failure. They exaggerate failure potential in their minds, convincing themselves that every move entails a high degree of risk. If you harbor this fear, you should think about some of the decisions that you made in the past that led to success. With hindsight, you'll realize that in each instance, you took a chance and it paid off. If you're a CEO or any type of top executive, you've probably built up a great deal of leadership equity because of your success. This gives you a certain leeway to make mistakes. Use it!

• *Confront your worst fears.* We've found that overly cautious leaders subconsciously deny their imagined worst-case scenarios. In other words, they don't articulate to themselves the real reason they're being so stubbornly indecisive. They don't allow themselves to say, even in their private thoughts, "I'm refusing to make a decision about this acquisition because I know of other companies where the costs have dragged them into bankruptcy, and that's what I think might happen to us." When you make this fear conscious, you lessen its power. Don't misunderstand: The fear of bankruptcy may be realistic. But the upside of the acquisition may outweigh the possibility of bankruptcy, and you can catalyze action when bringing the worst-case scenario out of the back of your mind. Bringing it into the open loosens its hold on you. It's the same principle as encouraging a terrified child who can't go back to sleep to talk about a nightmare. Once articulated, it loses its power and the child can rest peacefully.

The Nice Guy Syndrome

A lot of overly cautious leaders are genuinely compassionate, friendly, and ethical individuals. They care so much about their companies and the people who work in them that they don't want to make an error that can hurt stockholders and employees. This doesn't mean that nice guys can't finish first. It just means that they need to be aware that their good impulses can have negative consequences. The impulse to be overly cautious makes perfect sense in some situations, but it can be a derailer when it stymies decision making.

Chris Galvin, the head of Motorola, is by all accounts a great guy. Smart, friendly, and knowledgeable about business, he gives people responsibility and is respected for it. But when it comes to making the big decisions, he seems hesitant. Though he has publicly disagreed with people who accuse him of being indecisive and makes a good case for being prudent, significant evidence exists that he is reluctant to pull the trigger. For a long time, he did not move fast enough to contain escalating costs. He spent months and even years searching for solid replacements for executives who had left key positions. And he was slow to introduce new products, allowing competitors to be first to market in categories that were Motorola's core business. Motorola has lost significant market share over the past few years, and many wonder if the company can ever recapture its once-unassailable leadership position.

What's so tough with this derailer is that leaders can come up with all sorts of reasons for "watching and waiting" or "analyzing all the data." In one interview, Galvin said that he could decide quickly when "all the questions are answered." In this environment, and especially in Motorola's industry, speed is so critical that there often isn't time to hear all the questions, much less answer them. No doubt, Galvin was worried about the risk of acting before all the facts were in. On the other hand, Motorola has had to cut twenty-six thousand jobs in the past few years, undoubtedly a painful move for someone who inherited his father's legacy. How much worse would it have been if he had made decisions faster? Motorola has finally started making major changes that could turn things around in the coming years.

If overly cautious is your derailer, you should be aware of this truism: Almost all CEOs who have led a major change initiative, restructuring, or transformation have made the same observation: They wished they moved faster and sooner. All the factors that led them to go slowly seem trivial when they look back on what took place. They realize they could have accomplished more if they had simply had the courage of their convictions and pushed hard for change. Most of our clients talk about how much precious time was lost because of ambiguous fears of what could happen—and that if they had to do it all over again, they would move much more quickly to do what they knew had to be done.

We tell you this not to advocate reckless decision making or to suggest that the risks aren't real, but to help you take the steps necessary to manage this derailer.

CHAPTER FIVE

Habitual Distrust

You Focus on the Negatives

In his research on dysfunctional leadership, Professor Robert Hogan cites the example of CIA Director James Angleton, who was convinced that a mole had infiltrated his organization. He proceeded to wreak havoc in the agency by subjecting everyone to intense scrutiny. Through his policies, he cast a wide net of suspicion that disrupted work and hurt morale. He was eventually fired for these disruptive policies.

Interestingly, Angleton's suspicions were correct; it was later discovered that a mole (Aldrich Ames) had indeed infiltrated the CIA. Being right, though, doesn't always prevent failure. If you don't manage your disruptive impulses, being right may not matter.

Richard Nixon was well known as a distrustful leader. While it would be simplistic to suggest that this was the only factor in his derailment, it certainly contributed to it. Distrust caused him to tape his conversations; it gave rise to the creation of a "hit list" of political enemies; it encouraged him to unlawfully seek information on the activities of his adversaries and prevented him from forming partnerships that could have helped him accomplish more than he did.

In today's environment, it's not surprising that CEOs and other executives fall victim to this derailer. There is much to be suspicious of these days. Given the accounting and financial scandals that have disrupted many companies and the requirement to vouch for the veracity of quarterly financial reports, it is not surprising to find many CEOs, CFOs, and other executives scrutinizing internal financial reports and requiring others to attest to their accuracy, before signing themselves. Given the litigious workplace, regulatory requirements, potential product safety challenges, and complex licensing agreements, it would be unusual if people weren't wary of what might go wrong.

There is a difference, however, between healthy skepticism and virulent distrust. The former involves being realistic, reacting appropriately to circumstance and environment. The latter involves being inappropriately and egregiously suspicious. The leader who is consistently distrustful sends a message that people had better watch their backs rather than their work. Failure comes because people don't take risks under that steely gaze. They don't believe in themselves because the distrustful leader seems not to believe in them.

Distrust is one of those derailers that can manifest itself in many different ways. The next section looks at three of them.

Three Ways to Sabotage Your Career and Your Company

Before relating the following three cases, we should make it clear that none of these executives are paranoid in the clinical sense of the term. They're not distrustful to the point that they're always looking over one shoulder and seeing conspiracies in every gathering of employees that doesn't include them. Rather, their distrustful behavior arises under very specific circumstances. Unfortunately, it surfaces enough that it becomes a derailer.

Craig, for instance, was president of a division of a national retailer. He was known as "an excellent operator" in the retail business, and had a command of profit-and-loss trade-offs, consumer behavior, pricing, inventory, and markdowns. Craig grasped the downside of decisions before making them and always took great care to avoid this downside. His problem, however, was the weak team with which he surrounded himself. Ironically, Craig recognized the importance of having a strong staff and made a great effort to avoid selecting any weak players. His distrust, however, resulted in the very outcome that he was trying to avoid. His company had a strong corporate human resources group and a good process for executive recruitment and promotion. Craig dutifully used this process to screen candidates when positions opened. When looking over his initial list of names, though, Craig became skeptical. More than that, he was convinced that there was something wrong with the people on the list because he distrusted the process. He didn't have a solid rationale for this distrust—he had not experienced any major problems because of it—but his gut told him that the list was wrong. Why would people appear on this list? What was the real reason they were being offered up? So before Craig made any hiring or promotion decisions, he consulted a few trusted allies and asked them who they'd recommend for his opening. As a result, he often went outside the corporate succession process and hired and promoted from a very small pool of talent. In a number of instances, the people he hired lacked the skills or track record necessary for the position. Over a period of two or three years, Craig's division's performance deteriorated because his Executive Committee was soon made up of average but trustworthy performers.

Sara, on the other hand, exhibited a subtler form of distrust. An entrepreneur and founder of her own catalog company, Sara was the sort of CEO who assumes that no one in the company cares about work as much as the boss does. Unconsciously, she was always looking for evidence that people were slacking off or making decisions out of self-interest rather than for the good of the company. That's why she frequently popped unannounced into meetings or vigorously questioned people about why they wanted to make a particular move. She subtly investigated who came in on the weekend, how phones were being used, and whether expense accounts reflected true corporate activity. Sara wasted a great deal of time and energy trying to justify her distrust, but when catalog sales dropped, she immediately saw it as evidence that people were slacking off rather than of her own inability to confidently set a direction and trust others to execute it.

Tom, general counsel for a Fortune 100 corporation, became highly distrustful during times of stress. Most of the time, he was able to manage this derailer, and his healthy skepticism served him well as a lawyer and advocate for the company. But when he was called upon to work out contracts for critical deals or there was a lot of pressure to get a deal done, he turned trivial issues into major, deal-breaking problems. Everyone recognized that Tom was a terrific lawyer, but he rubbed people the wrong way when he started obsessing about minutiae and saw disaster around every corner. Tom killed many deals because of his irrational fears about potential problems, and line executives in the divisions complained loudly about his deal record. Tom's career unraveled as he struggled with finding the line between irrational distrust and healthy criticism.

Distrust has a particularly insidious effect when the CEO possesses this trait. Distrustful CEOs can easily create Nixonian environments where suspicion spreads from one executive to the next like a virus until it becomes an organization-wide derailer. In competitive environments in which companies must move quickly, operate globally and virtually, and incorporate diverse people and ideas, cultures of distrust can't survive. The company leader who only completely trusts the inner circle, those who "weren't acquired but grew up here" or those with similar functional backgrounds, operates with a severe handicap. The distrustful leader today is faced with the opportunity to use technology to monitor people's behavior (cameras, phone records, e-mail trails, and so on) and the need to fully trust others. Ironically, the higher an executive ascends the corporate hierarchy, the greater the need to trust and rely on others. The leader who creates layer upon layer of watchdog bureaucratic policies (unreasonable rules about personal phone use, overreactive punishments for minor rule infractions, inspection of irrelevant data about behavior) and who frequently articulates doubts about people may create a comprehensive self-fulfilling prophecy of betrayal.

Have You Crossed the Line?

You may have heard the expression, "Just because you're paranoid doesn't mean someone isn't following you." Distrust is appropriate at times and especially in certain professions. For instance, good lawyers have to watch for pitfalls and traps. But when they start raising red flags at the drop of a hat—as Tom did—then they cross the line. The following will help you determine which side of the line you're on:

You assess the potential downside before making a decision.	You never take action because you always see the downside.
You're alert for people whose actions are motivated by politics or self-interest.	You're constantly looking for confirmation that people are acting out of self-interest or for political reasons.
You can tolerate negative feedback and learn from it on occasion.	You dismiss all negative info on assumption that it's tainted by an individual's ulterior motives.
You mix criticism with positive comments when giving feedback to direct reports.	You're consistently critical when giving feedback.
You anticipate obstacles that can get in your way.	You obsess over what can go wrong.

Signs and Symptoms

Distrustful leaders have a difficult time recognizing their distrust as a derailer. In many cases, this lack of recognition results from their failure to accept feedback. A coach, a boss, or a mentor may

level with them and explain that their suspicious nature is causing them serious problems, but they're likely to dismiss this feedback by ascribing it to the source's personal agenda. As one
distrustful CEO responded to a consultant who was telling him
that his paranoia was alienating his executives: "That's because
no one else is capable of seeing the problems we may face."

Therefore, be aware that you may reflexively rationalize or
deny the signs and symptoms of a distrustful leader. Try to maintain your objectivity when considering if any of the following
attitudes or actions apply to you:

- *Relentless skepticism about other people's motives.* In any
organization, people exist who are only out for themselves. But if
this colors your thinking to the point that you question everyone
all the time about their decisions and actions, then you're going
to alienate people and prevent them from building the confidence necessary to take good risks. If you're always asking people
for more evidence before you lend them your support, or if you
frequently question their reasons for doing something, then
you're exhibiting this symptom of distrust.

- *Direct reports are highly defensive.* Pay attention to how
your people present ideas and reports to you. Are they constantly
covering themselves and seemingly afraid to commit to anything
until you give your approval? Are they justifying their actions or
concepts in anticipation of your response? When people have distrustful bosses, they expend enormous amounts of energy trying
to anticipate reactions. They play it safe in presentations, unwilling to risk all the questioning and skepticism they anticipate from
a distrustful boss. If this is how your people react to you, you're
placing a negative sanction on bold, cutting-edge thinking.

- *Difficulty forging alliances with outside groups or companies.* What has happened when you've attempted to partner with a vendor or work closely with any external group—a community organization, a trade association, a consultant? If distrust is a derailer for you, you've probably experienced a rough time on a number of occasions. Distrust often kicks into high gear when outsiders are involved. Whereas you might give an internal group the benefit of the doubt, outsiders are much harder to trust (distrustful leaders have a terrible time partnering with competitors on mutually beneficial projects). Like the worst sort of jingoist, you've divided the world into us and them, and the latter are automatically seen as untrustworthy.

Use Logic to Prevent Failure

Distrustful leaders tend to be highly logical people; this is a great strength. Though their distrust is illogical, they rely heavily on facts and figures and are skilled at compiling and analyzing information. We've found that people with this derailer often respond to well-reasoned arguments about how their distrust is hurting their companies and their careers.

That's why the following steps help prevent failure in distrustful leaders.

- *Analyze the "why" behind the distrust.* If you're distrustful, it's quite possible that you've never really examined the underlying reasons for your distrust. Instead, you've operated on a set of surface assumptions like "People will take advantage of me if I let them" and "If something can go wrong, it will go wrong." If you can find the cause of these assumptions, you will find it easier to moderate them. Psychologists know that people who are distrustful often experienced great disappointment or betrayal in childhood. When people reflect on some of these experiences, they find it easier to loosen the hold distrust has on them. They grasp that their distrust is illogical and has little to do with their relationships as adults.

• *Reconfigure a key relationship.* Choose someone you work closely with—usually a direct report or a boss—and examine the cause of your suspicions. Why do you doubt the other person's motives? Is there a real cause for distrust? Then consider the worst thing that might happen if you give the other person the benefit of the doubt on occasion. Finally, think about how you would feel if this individual reciprocated your feelings—and constantly questioned your actions and looked over your shoulder. Use the knowledge gained from these activities to change the way you interact with this person.

• *Practice giving positive feedback.* Distrust is a derailer when people reflexively look at worst-case scenarios, especially in scenario building and strategic planning. Forcing yourself to consider the best case, or an opportunity that might emerge from an action, gets you out of the habit of always looking at the dark side.

• *Recognize how distrust is hurting your career.* This step might not work for people suffering from the other derailers, but if distrust is your Achilles' heel, you are probably adept at analyzing situations. Think about what is happening or has happened to other distrustful executives in your organization. Companies are desperate for top executives who are able to work well with a wide range of people, who can catalyze great albeit risky ideas from direct reports and who are skilled at building partnerships with outsiders. If you have CEO or other top executive aspirations, then your distrustful nature will work against you. Again, logical analysis will help you moderate your distrustful tendency.

Trained to Be Distrustful

We'd like to share one final thought about people who work in fields where distrust is a prized trait. Accountants, attorneys, financial professionals, and policemen work in areas where a certain amount of distrust is necessary. None of us want an attorney who believes everything an opposing attorney says or a stockbroker who invests our money in a company that rumor says is going to do well. To some extent, all companies frown on executives who are so gullible and naive that they never see problems until it's too late. Distrust, though, can change from a realistic response to a given situation into a consistent attitude, and that's when it causes trouble. Even lawyers need to know when to manage their suspicions so they can reach settlements. Managing distrust, as opposed to letting it manage you, is the key to this derailer.

Perhaps Harvey Pitt, the former chairman of the Securities and Exchange Commission, learned this lesson. Pitt, who resigned after little more than a year on the job and under heavy criticism for partisanship, seemed like the perfect choice for SEC chairman. He knew the industry as only a true insider could, and by all accounts he is a brilliant lawyer. Upon taking the job, he was widely hailed as the perfect choice by politicians and professionals of nearly every persuasion. Although he was often described as arrogant, he also seems to have exhibited a number of behaviors associated with the distrust derailer that contributed to his short tenure.

The widely publicized final straw was his selection of William H. Webster to head a new accounting board over another candidate who was allegedly disliked by the accounting profession. Pitt's rejected candidate was also favored by his predecessor, which seems to have catalyzed Pitt's opposition. It also turned out that Pitt failed to inform other SEC commissioners that Webster had been involved with a company that had been accused of fraud. To investigate Webster before he was appointed, Pitt relied on an old friend who hadn't done this type of investigation before rather than someone he could count on to be thorough and tough.

Before this final episode, there had been a number of other incidents. For instance, it was reported that Pitt had privately lobbied to have his job elevated to Cabinet-level status, even though he had been advised that this was a bad idea by a veteran SEC executive. Instead, he apparently relied on a small group of advisers who didn't grasp the political implications of such lobbying and how it would anger Democrats and the White House.

If you look at the behaviors associated with distrustfulness—skepticism about other people's motives, defensive direct reports, withholding information from others, difficulty in forging alliances with outsiders—you see evidence of them in stories reporting Pitt's turbulent time as SEC chairman. It's instructive that an individual as ideally suited to a job as Pitt could ultimately fail. Too often, we assume that someone whose professional background is a perfect fit for a job—who has the ideal combination of intellectual acumen, experience, and expertise—cannot fail. The lesson: Never underestimate the power of personality in undermining the success of even the most brilliant and well-suited leader.

CHAPTER SIX

Aloofness

You Disengage and Disconnect

W—hen you think of the aloof CEO, the image conjured is of the cerebral official in a secretary-guarded office who emerges only to consult with a few trusted executives. Smart and dispassionate, the aloof CEO generally succeeds by analytical rather than people skills. In the old-fashioned sense of the term, this is a leader who can rise above the fray to make cool-headed, fiercely rational decisions.

Being aloof has its advantages. CEOs of this bent usually don't get caught up in politics or messy people problems. They're all business, which means they're rarely accused of playing favorites. People often feel confident in aloof leaders because such leaders seem to know what they're doing and are dedicated to doing it well.

When aloof leaders are under stress, though, they often become withdrawn. This is where things go off course. When they isolate themselves during crises or retreat from people who are desperately in need of their guidance, they are likely to fail. Of course, they don't see these aloof behaviors as a problem. We worked with a CEO who readily admitted he was aloof but said it was "just part of my personality." He was unaware that this trait cut him off from emotional relationships with others—which would have inspired commitment on their part. He also missed out on rich sources of ideas and thus became overly reliant on a narrow range of information.

Before we introduce you to two CEOs whose aloofness under stress caused problems, we should emphasize that this derailer is often mistaken for arrogance—but the two are different. You can be aloof without being arrogant. Aloof leaders may be perceived as excessively proud and egotistical when they are simply withdrawn or even shy. While arrogant CEOs will usually rely exclusively on personal judgment, aloof CEOs tend to trust a small inner circle—and that can create a different set of problems.

Why Aloof Leaders Experience Trouble in Tough Times

If you're a history buff, you might recall that FDR was a great leader for a country in the grip of the Depression and during WWII. Though he had a patrician background, he projected the image that he was a man of the people, that he cared. His Fireside Chats and warm manner of speech were reassuring during this difficult era. People want someone they can connect with during periods of uncertainty.

The same holds true in organizations. A few years ago, Rick Thoman was appointed CEO of Xerox, and he lasted in the job all of thirteen months. During his brief tenure, the company's stock and earnings dropped precipitously—and his leadership style was part of the cause, though there were certainly other factors that contributed to Xerox's problems. Thoman, described in the press as "aloof and cerebral," had done well as a top executive at American Express and IBM, but he made mistakes at Xerox that might have been caused by his aloofness. For instance, his reorganization of the company's sales force distanced some of

Xerox's top salespeople from their customers. His inability to manage the role of Paul Allaire, the former CEO who remained as chairman, contributed to his difficulties. Perhaps if Thoman had been in better touch with key sales leaders, he might have anticipated the risks and resistance that a sales force reorganization typically induces. When you're an aloof CEO, you're cutting yourself off from the key currency of the realm—people, ideas, and information, and this might have been among the reasons Thoman failed.

Steve Case is another former CEO who has been described as aloof. Articles describing his leadership style after the merger of Time Warner and AOL have emphasized his unwillingness or inability to connect with other people on a personal level, and his withdrawal from active involvement in AOL Time Warner, which led to his resignation.

Josh, CEO of a spectacularly successful software company we know, was much younger than Thoman but no less aloof. Josh's technological genius and brilliant grasp of the software market fueled the company's growth. For three years, the organization grew rapidly, and Josh orchestrated the growth by developing great new products to meet an ever-increasing demand. Then the bottom fell out. The dot-com crash, technology industry implosion, and reduced capital spending combined with a giant software company's knockoffs of Josh's innovative products to create serious problems for his company. Many of the employees were young and had never experienced this type of sudden downturn. Naturally, they looked to Josh for reassurance and to give them hope for the future. Josh, though, was unable to give it to them.

In the best of times, Josh wasn't the sort who enjoyed socializing; he felt most comfortable in front of his computer or discussing strategy with the three other people with whom he started the company. Interestingly, most of Josh's employees wouldn't have characterized him as aloof during the company's boom years. He was shy, certainly, and perhaps a bit of a loner, but he never talked down to anyone and always enjoyed receiving input and responding to it (though he preferred interoffice e-mail for this purpose).

It was only in a crisis that Josh retreated into his office and rarely emerged. People noted the change in his demeanor and worried that it was a bad sign for the company. They also worried when he stopped returning people's phone calls and e-mail messages. It wasn't that Josh was intentionally distancing himself from his managers or going into a depression-induced shell. Instead, he was burying himself in his work, retreating into his computer and doing analysis after analysis of the market and how he might salvage what was left of the company's strategy. He just never thought about reassuring his people or making them part of the problem-solving process—actions that might have helped him through the crisis.

What Josh should have been doing, of course, was connecting with his managers, soliciting their ideas and encouraging them to hang in there with him. Because he didn't do these things, some of his best talent soon departed for other jobs, leaving the company without sufficient talent when the market picked up. Ultimately, Josh was forced to merge his company with a much larger competitor at an unattractive price.

Have You Crossed the Line?

Aloofness becomes a derailer when it isolates you from key internal and external people. Many high-performing CEOs have been described as shy, intellectual, diffident, solitary, and in other terms suggestive of aloofness, but they achieved greatness because they were able to manage their derailer. Though they never became world-class relationship builders, they were aware of their tendencies and took steps to moderate them to avoid getting themselves or their companies in trouble. Use the following to see if your aloof attitude has caused you to cross to the failure side of the line:

You create an environment where decisions are made objectively and politics is rarely played.	You create a "cold" culture where expression of feeling is frowned upon.
You're calm in the midst of crisis and controversy.	You withdraw in the midst of crisis and controversy.
You maintain an outward reserve but can connect with people when necessary.	You're stoic to the point that you never show anyone your weaknesses or open yourself up to others.
You delegate most relationship-building activities to others but are willing to forge key alliances in crucial situations.	You're unable to work in teams or create alliances.

Signs and Symptoms

The signs of aloofness-caused failure are usually clear and unmistakable. They include

• *Becoming invisible.* Everyone has a story about some top executive or CEO they worked for who never seemed to emerge from the corner office during a difficult time for the company; as rumors flew and the company sank, this leader became a shadowy figure, seeming to come and go at odd hours so as not to have to deal with people demanding answers to tough questions. While this type of deliberate invisibility may be an extreme example of how an aloof leader acts, it demonstrates a very common tendency to withdraw during a crisis. Other related symptoms might include scheduling numerous out-of-town trips, customer visits, or location reviews, or finding other excuses for being out of the office when people are under pressure and need personal support.

• *Ignoring conflict.* Conflict is emotionally difficult, and aloof leaders have a hard time dealing with strong feelings. If you see yourself ignoring a battle between your direct reports or hoping that it will go away on its own, failure may be right around the corner. Aloof CEOs who allow differences among executives to go unresolved risk losing valuable people as well as creating a culture of simmering animosity. They rationalize that the highly paid executives who work for them should be able to resolve their differences, or that they "expect grownups to work through their differences." In the worst cases, leaders beset by this derailer may not even be aware that conflict exists. They unconsciously screen out all conflict because they don't want to confront it. And people around them learn to do the same thing.

- *People stop working hard.* When CEOs are aloof, they run the risk of taking away a nonfinancial incentive for performance. With no pats on the back (or not enough of them), no celebration of goals achieved, and no rewarding emotional connection, people ask themselves, "Why am I working this hard?" Many times, people work hard because they feel a top executive is depending on them. They come in on weekends or wrestle with a tough issue because they have a relationship with the CEO and want to honor that relationship. On the other hand, accomplished, successful, highly paid executives complain bitterly when working for an aloof CEO who cannot manage to cough up a compliment. If you're aloof, your emotional connections with most people in the company may be tenuous at best and you may not be motivating them to work at full capacity.

- *False assumptions and miscommunication run rampant.* Because it's difficult to talk to someone who is aloof, people tend to act on guesses about what such a CEO wants. Lacking the easy access necessary to clarify a directive, the CEO's direct reports make assumptions about what their boss meant by that memo or that obscure pronouncement during a meeting. Execution suffers, a particular problem for aloof CEOs who have brilliant ideas but lack the ability to communicate them clearly.

- *Lack of cultural passion.* In some companies, you can feel the excitement and energy just by walking the halls. You can't pass a conference room without seeing people fiercely debating an issue or an office without hearing an animated discussion. People exude passion and celebrate victory while damning the competition. Aloof CEOs dampen this passion. Their detached leadership style sends the message that displays of emotion are discouraged. Their communication style, whether in person or via memos, phone calls, and e-mail notes, has a clinical detachment that doesn't encourage personal conviction. Some people unconsciously mimic the aloof CEO's style. Others simply lose their enthusiasm for the hunt. The "people stop working harder" symptom combines with "people stop working with commitment." There's no sense of urgency or dedication to achieving certain outcomes. Passion often results in great ideas and great implementation, and without it, the odds of failure increase.

Avoiding Failure By "Staying in the Game"

When we coach aloof executives and talk to them about opening up and establishing more relationships, they sometimes resist because the challenge is so daunting. They often believe they don't have time for "that soft stuff," and that human connections are not what business is all about. If aloofness is a derailer for you, you may have a similar reaction. Be assured, therefore, that the changes we're going to suggest will allow you to retain a certain reserve and privacy. After all, CEOs with reputations for being aloof—Ken Lewis of Bank of America, for example—have been enormously successful. Consciously or not, they've learned how to prevent this trait from sabotaging their leadership, and you can learn the same lesson by addressing your aloofness at personal and organizational levels.

Personal

Here the goal is to let another person know a little bit more about who you are. You need to give other key executives some insight about what makes you tick. It may be as simple as letting someone know when you're angry or pleased. It may involve sharing your enthusiasm for a particular accomplishment or your disappointment about a missed opportunity or a mistake. Practicing giving someone else insight about who you are will moderate the impact of your aloofness. If you do it consistently, it will increase the chance that you'll establish more meaningful relationships with more people. It will also get you in the habit of loosening up on occasion, humanizing your leadership style to the point that you'll be less likely to wall yourself up in your office during a crisis.

Be aware that you probably set boundaries in your professional life that make this step difficult. We've found that aloof CEOs, especially, believe that they have to separate the personal and the professional to be effective; that allowing other people at work to see their private side will make it more difficult to maintain respect and keep the distance necessary to maintain objectivity. Many older executives have moved up through the ranks with this theory in mind, but it's no longer valid. In a relationship-driven world, leaders need to connect with people, which is why we're suggesting you practice connecting in small ways.

We also want to assure you that you're capable of sharing aspects of yourself with people you work with. Contrary to what some people think, just because you're aloof doesn't mean you lack feelings (or that you are a less feeling person than others). It's just that you don't communicate them. Aloof leaders need to work on being more transparent.

Organizational

Though most aloof leaders won't admit it, they are somewhat naive about how organizations get things done today. Small networks of influence within companies accomplish much more than any single individual can, no matter how powerful. Aloof leaders fail because they aren't part of these networks and don't know how to use them. The following exercises will help you manage this failure factor:

- *Map out your network.* Identify who should be in it to accomplish your goals. Who do you need as allies, who controls the resources you require, who has critical veto power and who can provide the green light? This may seem like a daunting task at first, and you may need to ask a politically astute colleague for assistance. This process, though, is a great way to start becoming more savvy about how things really work within your company. We frequently ask clients to construct a "political map of the territory," and they are astounded to realize the influence networks they ignore.

- *Rehearse your messages.* What message do you want to send to a particular individual? What do you really want someone to understand about the importance of a project or how achieving a certain objective will affect the organization? Part of the problem that aloof leaders have is motivating others—they may communicate what they want someone to do without paying attention to the why and how. Some people need pep talks while others need the opportunity to ask you questions. Rehearse in your mind the best approach given the other person's needs.

- *Pay attention to your impact.* Or rather, pay attention to your lack of impact. Watch for blank stares and other indications that you're not getting through to someone. People may not understand where you stand on an issue or where a task is on your list of priorities. You need to be more transparent with your expectations so that you get people's heads nodding and you see the light of understanding appear in their eyes. To do this, you may have to have a longer conversation than you usually do or be more emphatic when making your points. When we coach aloof leaders, we often end up telling them something along the lines of, "You know, I don't have the vaguest idea what you're thinking right now. I've been offering you a suggestion, and you could be thinking this is the greatest idea in the world or that I'm just blowing smoke."

While no one except a coach or a boss is going to talk to you in this manner, try and read your direct reports and colleagues to see if your message is really connecting.

Beware of Aloof Cultures

One tricky aspect of this derailer is that some corporate cultures reflect this aloof quality. In some companies, people routinely work behind closed doors, you never hear a raised voice, and it's considered bad form to emote in any significant way. The hushed, quiet feeling in the corridors makes you feel like you're working in a library.

If this describes your company's culture—and if you as CEO helped create it—you're not going to change yourself or the company overnight. Rather than just accept this aloof environment as a given, however, you should work at making incremental changes. If you can loosen up your behavior a bit and be more transparent, others will eventually follow suit. If you don't, expect to be blindsided. Aloof cultures historically are hit by developments that they should have seen coming but didn't. Competitive forays, changes in the regulatory environment, and economic shifts are just some of the things aloof organizations fail to anticipate because of their limited sources of information. Don't let your organization be blindsided because of its self-imposed and unintentional isolation.

CHAPTER SEVEN

Mischievousness

You Know That Rules
Are Only Suggestions

Despite the serious, professional demeanor of many CEOs, below the surface often lurks a mischievous quality that represents enormous creativity and a capacity to see things differently—but can also derail careers faster than a financial scandal. In fact, it may be the cause of at least some of the financial scandals that have recently plagued many companies in the news. Mischievous leaders often act impulsively and don't consider the impact of their actions; they may become so caught up in the cleverness of their ideas that they don't assess the ramifications. Relatively few mischievous CEOs are white-collar criminals. Most are law-abiding citizens, and their impulse to break the rules, to test the limits and shake people up, can serve them and their organizations well. Their willingness to challenge the status quo in their organizations and thumb their noses at tradition are terrific leadership traits that redefine industries and establish market leadership.

Former President Clinton was a mischievous leader, and it allowed him to reconceptualize government and redefine his constituencies. Like many people with this trait, he had enough charm to defuse the negative impact of many of his gambits. Ultimately, however, his mischievous nature tarnished his legacy because, unconsciously at least, he was convinced that the rules didn't apply to him.

This type of leader is a second cousin to the eccentric, in that both take great pleasure in provocative ideas and both can have trouble executing these ideas. The big difference between the two, though, is that eccentric leaders often come across as odd or strange, while mischievous leaders are much more charming and engaging.

If you're this type of leader, you're courting failure when you don't think through the consequences of your impulsive, spontaneous rule-breaking actions. Because you know you can charm, persuade, and effectively cajole people, you act, and only with hindsight do you realize you should have thought before you acted.

Rebels Without a Cause

Mischievous behavior at the CEO level often best shows up in accounting scandals and investor lawsuits—the many financial control mechanisms cannot easily be circumvented and tend to bring mischievous decision making to light. Although many companies such as Qwest, Xerox, and Tyco have had to restate earnings to make up for questionable accounting practices, WorldCom and Waste Management are two good examples of companies that, with the cooperation of the CFO and probably the CEO, actually bent accounting rules to depreciate assets outside normal accepted practice. In the case of Waste Management, led by CEO Michael Buntrock, depreciation schedules were unusually stretched out— lowering annual depreciation charges and boosting earnings. In some cases, Buntrock and his team kept two sets of books— imposing the questionable depreciation schedules at headquarters on assets that were valued properly in the field. At WorldCom, Bernie Ebbers and Scott Sullivan allegedly conspired to account for assets as expenses in mischievous, nonstandard practices designed to inflate earnings.

Michael Cowpland, the former CEO of Canada's Corel Corp., looked to all the world like the sort of brash, rule-breaking, idea-generating leader who thrives in the software industry. Corel, Canada's largest software company, acquired WordPerfect in 1996 in an attempt to take on Microsoft's dominant products. Cowpland initially generated much media attention and enthusiasm. He invested heavily in Java when it seemed it might overtake Windows, and after that Cowpland adapted WordPerfect to Linux systems, thinking there would be a big market there.

None of this worked. But Cowpland kept generating ideas—ideas that at first seemed revolutionary and with the potential of generating huge profits. At one point, Cowpland orchestrated what seemed to be a wise merger with Inprise Corp., but Inprise decided not to go through with it upon learning that Corel had experienced a major operating loss. Cowpland launched idea after idea, but many of them were implemented without sufficient planning or support and never amounted to much.

While Cowpland was an exciting CEO and the media enjoyed covering him, debt kept mounting and the company's main business—graphics software—was neglected in favor of Cowpland's new ideas. He resigned without any of his major strategic concepts ever making money for the company.

Now we'd like to tell you of another senior executive we worked with recently. Joe, a division head of a large corporation, picked us up at the airport and proceeded to drive us to another company's headquarters, where we were scheduled to attend a half-day meeting. When we arrived, though, all the parking spaces in the lot were filled. There was another lot about a block away, and we assumed

Joe would drive over to that one and we could walk back together to the headquarters building. Instead, he pulled into a spot in front of a large sign marked "VISITORS—10 MINUTE PARKING ONLY."

"What about the sign?" we asked him.

"What sign are you talking about?" he asked, as he maneuvered the car into the spot.

When we questioned him about this action, Joe explained that he knew that the ten-minute visitor spaces never filled up, that he was familiar with the patrol patterns of corporate security, and that the importance of the meeting and the need to be on time more than justified parking in the space. What Joe was really saying was that he was more important than the parking lot rule, which made perfect sense to him. Joe was a highly successful leader who had broken a number of rules over the course of his career. Until we began working with him, he didn't grasp that this reflexive rule-breaking might eventually lead to failure.

Karen also didn't grasp this concept. A brilliant young strategist at one of the world's largest companies, she had been hotly pursued by a mid-sized corporation that offered her a top executive position and a promise that she'd be strongly considered for the CEO job when the current CEO retired in three years. Karen accepted the offer, and she did well during her first year, in part because she had a mandate to shake things up. Shake them up she did. Karen had astutely analyzed this company before agreeing to join it, and she felt that the company had tremendous potential because of its superior technology and strong R&D group. She also believed that the company was being held back by a "country club" culture where no one wanted to step on anyone's toes.

After her first year, a lot of the company's managers had sore feet. Karen confronted many poor performers and demanded results from her direct reports. More than one person said she was a "breath of fresh air." Karen's humor and charm defused the animosity that a less likable leader who made difficult decisions might have raised. Unfortunately, one person did react negatively to Karen's style: the company's largest customer—the president of that company, to be specific. During a tense session in which Karen's vice president of sales was attempting to explain a recent price hike, Karen interrupted and joked that the customers should consider themselves lucky that the price increase wasn't greater than it was, considering the enormous investment in research the company had made, and that "maybe they could ship some of last year's inventory if they wanted the 'blue light special.'"

Though Karen made these remarks as a light-hearted attempt at humor, the president of this customer's company didn't take them this way. His company had just gone through a difficult downsizing, he was sensitive about cost issues, and he expected more seriousness during the negotiation. Karen seemed insensitive, especially when she started joking that the customer's company might save some money if they sold their corporate jet and "started traveling by commercial jet like the rest of us penny-pinchers."

When this customer found another supplier, Karen was blamed. Though it's quite possible that the customer would have left anyway because of the price increase, the board of directors was well aware of Karen's comments during this fateful meeting. Whether she was a scapegoat or guilty as charged didn't matter.

The board's CEO succession committee eliminated Karen from its list of candidates.

Have You Crossed the Line?

As you consider whether your mischievous qualities are derailing your career or hurting your company, remember that this trait is worse than it sounds. Mischief may seem like a benign word, but at its worst it can create tremendous problems because consequences haven't been considered. Managing this derailer means knowing when you can be spontaneous and break the rules, and when you can't.

Here's a look at whether you are managing your mischievous instincts or have crossed the line:

You test limits and push at boundaries to foster innovation.	You break the rules because you believe rules are boring and unneccessary.
You are impulsively creative.	You are destructively impulsive.
You enjoy risk-taking and don't dwell on mistakes.	You make decisions and take risks without considering the consequences.
You use your charm and creativity to achieve organizational goals.	You use your charm and creativity as a matter of personal style and not to achieve specific goals.

You make provocative statements in order to foster debate and discussion.	You speak your mind for your own amusement or without any real objective.

×

Signs and Symptoms

Every organization needs some mischievous leaders. They're the ones who ask, Do we have to do things as we've always done them? Can we think of other ways of approaching this problem? They challenge and push people, fostering innovation and breakthrough thinking—and they often do these things with such wit and irreverence that people enjoy the push and challenge. In fact, mischievous CEOs generally have tremendously loyal followings. People want to work with leaders who are charismatic and daring.

A funny thing happens, though, when leaders become too mischievous. They alienate loyalists and come to be seen as gadflies and provocateurs rather than serious leaders. Failure occurs because the negative consequences of their actions start outweighing their inventiveness and charm.

See if the following warning signs apply to you:

- *People question your commitments and the projects you've started.* In the past year, you may have launched many exciting new programs and pledged your support to a variety of initiatives, but your support is short-lived. You've moved on to other projects and initiatives and left the earlier efforts to flounder. Not only does this confuse people, it tends to alienate those individuals within your company—as well as customers and clients outside—who value sustained excellence and continuity. It also can prematurely kill projects and teams that might have delivered great results if nurtured over a period of time.

- *You don't take the time to win people over.* Mischievous leaders aren't manipulators and schemers. Instead, they are seat-of-the-pants type leaders, acting on the spur of the moment and letting the chips fall where they may. They may disdain corporate procedure and processes, and rather than enroll people in new ideas or ways of doing things, they expect others to grasp the uniqueness of their ideas and positions. They expect people to fall in line, which sometimes happens. In other instances, though, people don't buy into their rule-breaking, tradition-busting ideas. Rather than try and use their considerable charm to carefully discuss, persuade, and sell them, they ignore the dissenters, or worse, label them as "change resistant." Sometimes they do so at their own peril.

- *Everything seems to rate a challenge.* In other words, you don't pick your battles. Perhaps you've received feedback from others to the effect that you can be a troublemaker. If you could read their thoughts, you'd hear them thinking, "What is that loon going to do next?" The devilish desire to stir things up can make others anxious, even frightened. You can see the grimaces when you talk about changing a policy you just changed or start talking about reorganizing a department after it was just reorganized. If doing things differently becomes a habit, you'd better break it or risk burning people out with your mini-rebellions.

- *You often find yourself finessing your mistakes.* Mischievous leaders are skillful at denying or covering up mistakes. Their eloquence can convince an audience that it wasn't really their fault even though it obviously was. They can deflect attention from themselves by raising another, more compelling issue, arguing over the meaning of words or their true intentions rather than actual consequences. Over time, however, these mistakes come back to haunt them because they don't deal with the issues head on. If you're prevaricating, obfuscating, and rationalizing consistently, look inward for a mischievous derailer.

• *You're easily bored.* Mischievous leaders like others to join in their fun. If they're not stirring the pot—if they're not creating a certain amount of commotion—they lose interest. To avoid being bored, they provoke conflicts or take potshots. Details often bore them more than anything else, so they ignore them, much to the company's peril. Mischievous managers are often poor at execution, because execution requires a certain amount of detail work, and details bore them. Another related symptom is impatience; they sometimes have short attention spans. This feeds into the earlier symptom of failing to develop people. If your eyes wander, you take important phone calls during meetings and conversations, or you're inspired to continually relate your own experiences when your direct reports try to talk with you, those direct reports are not going to develop confidence in their own contribution.

Managing Your Inner Mischief-Maker

When we've talked to mischievous CEOs about controlling their shake-things-up, ignore-the-consequences tendencies, we've been met with "Who, me?" responses. This leads us right into our first suggestion about how to manage this derailer:

• *Take ownership of what you're really doing.* This simply means acknowledging what's going on when you become a contrarian in meetings or when you start testing limits. In the case of the CEO who parked in the ten-minute visitors' spot, he needed to admit that he enjoyed demonstrating that the rules didn't apply to him. In the case of this CEO, we helped him own his behavior by asking the following questions:

Do you think there are other people who would abide by this rule and not park here?

Why do you feel you're different? What entitles you to break the rule?

Do you get a kick out of thumbing your nose at established procedures and policies?

What we're suggesting is that you question yourself about your rule-breaking, consequence-ignoring behaviors. By doing so, you can surface the real reasons you act mischievously and have a better chance of controlling these behaviors because you'll be conscious of them.

• *Determine which rules are important to follow.* CEOs and other top leaders often believe that they make the rules and others follow them. Because they make the rules, they rationalize, they should feel free to break them or make new ones. This logic is only valid up to a point. In reality, consistent rule-breakers lose respect. They are seen as not believing in anything except their own private agendas. They are also viewed as hypocritical, in that they don't walk the talk.

Mischievous leaders need to walk a fine line. You don't want to lose the mischievous quality that drives your charisma and your risk-taking. Managing it, though, means delineating what rules you will and won't break. Some leaders determine that they won't break any internal rules—the ones they help formulate and that their people have to live with. They will, however, break external rules such as those that govern partnerships in their industry or advertising strategies.

By satisfying your need to break rules, you make it easier to adhere to the rules that really matter.

• *Role-play being on the receiving end of mischief.* Role-playing isn't effective with all the derailers, but it can be very useful for this one. Mischievous executives don't grasp how their statements and actions will impact others. Because they say and do things impulsively, they don't consider the potential negative consequences. More than one mischievous leader has tossed off a series of wild ideas in an informal meeting only to be shocked when someone took the ideas as directives and acted on them.

Think about the ideas and actions you're going to be proposing and put yourself in the head of the direct report, customer, or other individual who will be most affected by it. Think about how you might respond if you were this person.

> Would you need some explanation or convincing before you accepted the idea and made a commitment to it?
>
> Would you have good reasons for feeling that what's being suggested violates the company's tradition or values?
>
> Would you need support and resources from other areas to have a chance of making the idea work?

Answering these questions will help you both determine whether an idea is realistic and how you should present it so that it has the best chance of being implemented successfully.

• *Confide in a coach.* While we believe coaching is useful for all eleven derailers (we admit to being biased in this regard), we've found it especially helpful for this one. Mischievous leaders are often oblivious to the impact they have on people and the business, and a coach can raise their consciousness in this regard. Being able to talk about whether a given action is likely to have a constructive or destructive effect can reduce the likelihood of committing destructive acts unknowingly. As much as their spontaneity and seat-of-the-pants leadership is a plus, mischievous leaders benefit greatly when they can call a time-out and confide what earth-shaking idea is percolating in their minds. What all this boils down to is that you need to confide in someone before you confound or confuse too many people.

A Daring Doll

When Mattel CEO Jill Barad resigned after the company lost $18.4 million in one quarter, she failed to live up to the organization's and industry's expectations. She had orchestrated the incredible success of the Barbie line of dolls, and her charisma and smarts made people think that her continued success might pave the way for other woman CEOs of Fortune 500 companies.

Barad seems to have exhibited the rule-breaking reflex central to this mischievous trait. Just by being one of four women who were Fortune 500 CEOs at the time, she was breaking the rules. Her management style and her strategies also challenged the conventional wisdom. She wore Barbie-bright outfits, and she would sometimes start dancing during business presentations. A number of male executives departed the company when she was the boss, complaining that she had trouble working with men. And she introduced flexible work hours and other new work style concepts.

In terms of strategies, Barad broke the rules when she revamped the Barbie line, moderating the doll's movie star image by creating Doctor Barbie dolls and other professional incarnations. Her last daring move—a $3.5 billion acquisition of the Learning Company, an educational software firm—was designed to make Mattel more than just a toy company, broadening its appeal with educational, high-tech products for children.

That this last move didn't pan out wasn't completely Barad's fault. A changing market hurt other companies as well. Nonetheless, Barad was criticized for not executing her last strategy as well as she might have. It's certainly fair to speculate that her mischievous qualities accelerated her fall from grace. As you'll recall, one of the symptoms of this derailer is not trying to win people over. It's possible that if Barad had made more of an effort to win over her male direct reports, she might not have lost as much talent as she did. It's also possible that her flashy outfits, dancing during presentations, and other provocative behaviors caused people not to give her the credit she deserved. Mischievous leaders are vulnerable to criticism of being superficial, of having a lot of style but not much substance.

Most people acknowledged that Barad was a great marketer, where mischievous traits come in handy. The criticism against her was that she didn't have what it took to be a great CEO. This might have been an illusion conjured by her mischievous tendencies, but it's one that resulted in the unpleasant reality of losing her job.

CHAPTER EIGHT

Eccentricity

It's Fun to Be Different
Just for the Sake of It

Eccentrics come in all shapes and sizes. We recently worked with a very well-known CEO who has an eight-foot-tall blow-up Fred Flintstone doll in his office. When this CEO was puzzled by an issue or attempting to manage a conflict, he would turn to the cartoon figure and say, "Let's see what Fred thinks about this."

Then there was the senior vice president of a major corporation who dressed to kill; her favorite outfit was a Dragon Lady costume and she also enjoyed draping herself in all types of furs, including one with the head of a small mammal still intact. She used language that could charitably be termed "salty" and was known to blast music in her office and sometimes dance by herself.

And we should mention the high-tech guru who lived in his office for days at a time, sometimes without showering or changing his clothes. The office floor was littered with carry-out containers and when he was in his intensive work mode, all his people could get out of him were monosyllabic responses. He insisted people call him "Chet" (not his real name) because it inspired his creativity.

These three individuals are obviously quite different from each other, but they all have incredibly fecund minds; ideas emerge from them with great speed and occasional brilliance. Their success is due in no small part to their ability to generate ideas and deliver results—or else others would not tolerate their weirdness.

At least it helps people tolerate these leaders in good times. Then they are viewed as true originals, and their strange behaviors are spoken of with a certain amount of affection. Eccentric CEOs are sometimes thought to be successful precisely because of their eccentricities. Ted Turner of AOL Time Warner; Richard Huber of Aetna; H. Ross Perot of Perot Systems, even Bill Gates of Microsoft come to mind as individuals who make a unique statement because of the way they do things. Their ability to see the business differently from others allows them to identify opportunities and openings; their ability to come up with unique approaches helps them take advantage of market openings that others dismiss.

When things aren't going so well, however, eccentrics become irritating. When everyone is pounding on their door during a crisis saying a decision has to be made, their tendency to float more ideas is frustrating. When a crisis unfolds, their "Let's see what Fred thinks" response can be maddening. Failure for eccentrics begins when they think instead of act, as the following examples demonstrate.

A Little Off the Beat:
The Problem with Marching to Your Own Drummer

We'd like to share two stories with you, the first of which took place in the mid-nineties, but has become an almost classic story of an eccentric CEO. Paul Kazarian took over as CEO of Sunbeam-Oster three years earlier, and his astute moves took the then $1 billion company out of bankruptcy and into the black. This was a legendary accomplishment. He gave his senior officers large bonuses, which would make it seem likely that they would support him.

In fact, they lobbied behind the scenes for his dismissal and achieved that goal when the board fired him. What had Kazarian done to deserve this unlikely failure? Here are some examples of his behavior during his tenure:

- Routinely chewed out his senior people and called one of them "scum."

- Made obscene comments to women.

- Smashed telephones.

- Threw a pint of orange juice at his controller.

- Shot a BB gun at empty chairs during a meeting while yelling, "Die!"

Admittedly, this is an extreme example of eccentricity, but it illustrates not only that truly weird individuals can become CEO but that once in the role they can be eccentric, deliver results, and sabotage themselves. The next story demonstrates how an eccentric leader can go off the rails in a less obviously crazy way.

Dennis was a top executive with a traditional manufacturing firm that had always focused on operational results. He'd been hired because the CEO loved the energy and innovation he'd demonstrated in previous jobs and thought that the company needed someone like Dennis. At first, things went well. His analysis of why a new product group wasn't performing up to expectations—and his suggestions about how to turn things around—helped the company enormously.

As Dennis became comfortable in his new environment, his eccentricities emerged. He decorated his office with posters of Plato, Einstein, and Freud. He peppered his conversation with allusions to quantum physics and the Romantic poets. At times, people found these behaviors amusing and intellectually stimulating. In certain situations, however, they were confused. Sometimes Dennis went off on irrelevant diatribes that were fun to listen to but distracted everyone from the matter at hand. Dennis also was highly impulsive. When meeting with a new team that he was managing, he suggested a direction, and the team promptly pursued it. After much time and effort, a team member discovered that their approach had already been tried by another team, and it had not worked. Dennis should have known this—he had all the reports of the previous team assigned to this project—but he'd ignored it. Even worse, Dennis would change his mind frequently. One day he'd come up with what he'd call "an idea of Einsteinian dimensions" and drum up great enthusiasm. The next day, he'd dismiss his brainstorm and float a completely different concept.

Dennis's ideas often had merit, but this method of unleashing them left a lot of people upset. Several senior executives complained to the CEO that Dennis was unfocused. A direct report Dennis inherited said he would be "a great leader in a sole proprietorship." What doomed Dennis, though, was that in a company that stressed quarterly operational results, Dennis had few to show. Aside from his initial success, few of the projects he led came through with positive outcomes. Though he tried to get a few new product ideas off the ground, he lacked the patience and skill to move them forward in a controlled, organized manner. It didn't help matters that Dennis had a reputation for being weird and made the more conservative members of management uncomfortable. For these reasons, he was eventually terminated.

Have You Crossed the Line?

In our increasingly diverse culture, people are growing more tolerant of eccentrics. We recognize that uniform standards of behavior may not be possible in a society that recognizes different lifestyles, values, and expressions of identity. Dress codes, linguistic rules, and social manners have been relaxed. In most companies, acceptance of individuals who don't fit the white male norm has increased. An emphasis on entrepreneurship and innovation has also made eccentricity more acceptable in large organizations. Given the success of technology start-ups that prize substance and ideas over style, corporations are looking to borrow a page from the start-up stories, and that often means promoting creative leaders who have entrepreneurial and business-building skills, including (in some instances) eccentricity.

At the same time, there is a difference, sometimes a fine line between innovation and complete ridiculousness—or between unbridled and managed eccentricity. The latter reduces eccentricity to an idiosyncrasy—a tolerable behavior. The former turns it into a dominant trait, causing people to become lost in their ideas and unable to get things done.

With that in mind, determine the side of the line you fall on:

You have a million great ideas.	You have a million great ideas that rarely get executed.
You keep people on their toes with your unpredictable and offbeat style.	You confuse and confound people with your style.

You've launched many important initiatives.	You've launched many initiatives but don't follow up on them.
————————×————————	
You blend your original and sometimes unconventional style with a more conforming approach when necessary.	You refuse to change who you are by conforming in any way to organizational norms.
————————×————————	

Signs and Symptoms

We know one prominent CEO who is very successful—but also not as successful as he could be because of his eccentric nature. His eccentricities are directly related to his creativity—but he derails himself and his organization in times of stress, especially market pressure. People in his company joke about his "twenty-seven key priorities," but it's not a joking matter. He's right— they're all important, but he can't focus himself or his team on the two or three most important ones. An inability to prioritize creates confusion or, even worse, leaves leaders and individual contributors spending too much time on less important business drivers. In fact, that is the first of our symptoms for this derailer.

• *Inability to prioritize.* The eccentric believes that each and every idea is critically important, and so becomes attached to them. In a very real sense, the ideas become the eccentric leader's children, and it doesn't seem right to favor one over another. The eccentric leader can hold forth about each of the many initiatives and projects these ideas have sparked. But the team can't figure out which one they should concentrate on because the leader is unable or unwilling to prioritize. The eccentric rationalizes this idea-juggling by thinking that the best one will "naturally" take precedence; that over time winning ideas will emerge. In most cases, this doesn't happen. And when, through a natural organizational sorting of ideas and possibilities, the right projects emerge, they are pursued too late. People look to senior leaders to guide them through strategic direction setting and prioritization about where to invest their time, energy, and resources. In most companies, especially given the broad range of technologies and product innovations, options are many and prioritizing is crucial, and eccentrics let their people down here.

• *Going it alone.* Being eccentric becomes a derailer when you can't collaborate effectively. Deeply eccentric leaders are stubborn individualists. It's not that they want to isolate themselves or believe they're better than others, but their eccentricity is like a force field that surrounds them, repelling those who try to get too close. They frequently need their privacy. While they're not really loners, eccentrics can appear that way to others and drive them away. They also enjoy playing with their ideas by themselves and this trait can also isolate them.

• *People don't take you seriously.* This may be a more difficult symptom to discern than the others. Eccentric CEOs who are failing often are viewed as a joke. They're not hated or seen as incompetent, but their eccentric behaviors communicate that they're not serious leaders. In many instances, this is solely because they are unpredictable, unfocused, or unable to execute. They cannot follow through consistently on great ideas and brilliant insights. To determine whether people take you seriously, think about the following questions:

Of the ten best ideas, concepts, or strategies you came up with in
the past year, how many have been implemented?

Do you know the five most important things you need to achieve
in the coming year? Could you list them immediately
without having to do any analysis? And have you communicated these priorities to your people?

Do you sense that people aren't really listening when you per-
orate about your favorite new idea? Do they fail to follow up
with you and ask how they can help you execute the idea?

Are you aware if people have given you a sarcastic nickname? Do
you suspect that a significant percentage of those you work
with are cynical about your words and actions?

The Challenge of Compromise

To help eccentrics avoid failure, the easy answer is to get them to
identify and limit their priorities and focus on executing their
best ideas. If you're an eccentric, however, you're going to resist
this suggestion. Whatever form your eccentricity takes, from your
mannerisms to your clothing to your way of communicating,
you're going to view it as who you are. It's what makes you distinct; it's a quality that you possess and others lack, and it has
helped you achieve what you've achieved thus far. You may even
see your eccentricity as synonymous with a charismatic leadership style—one that has evolved naturally from your personality.

All this may be true, which is why you're going to initially
resist executing ideas and limiting priorities. Subconsciously,
perhaps, you're going to respond to these suggestions by telling
yourself, "Listing three priorities is what a typical, uncreative
leader does. Spending a lot of time on implementation isn't my

strength. Besides, people will really think I've sold out if I do a 180-degree change and start acting like a traditional leader."

With this internal rationalization in mind, see if the following suggestions might help you move away from eccentric-catalyzed failure:

- *Determine the price you're willing to pay.* More than one eccentric leader has told us, "I don't want to conform and be like everyone else. This is who I am!" If this is your attitude, you have to ask yourself how much conformity you're willing to tolerate in order to achieve your goals. If you could move your company up from a market challenger to a market leader position, would you be willing to focus on putting a few key strategies into practice? This may mean you can't continue working odd hours with the door closed or delivering brilliant but unfocused talks whenever a direct report asks you a question. Learning to manage this derailer involves moderating what others perceive as excesses, and you need to figure out if this sacrifice is worth it.

Ask yourself what your goals are—both for the company and for yourself—and the likelihood of achieving them in this organization. It may be that the sacrifice is too great and the chance of achieving your goals too small. You may be part of a company whose culture can't accommodate your particular eccentric way of managing and leading. Some companies need institutional leaders, others require change agents. The latter is more in keeping with an eccentric mindset, so it could be that you're a round peg in a square hole and need to move on.

If, however, you feel your company can achieve great things with your leadership, you may be motivated to conform to a point.

- *Surround yourself with people who can execute your ideas.* This may seem like obvious advice, but eccentrics often surround themselves with people who love to play with ideas and become bored when they have to execute them. As a result, there are no results.

To avoid this failure trap, select your team with an eye toward execution. If you had to create specs for this team, the top one would be: "Ability to translate ideas into action." It may feel strange selecting direct reports who are your opposite in certain ways. You may feel much more comfortable with other idea people. But if you want to succeed in your organization, you'll bite the bullet and find individuals who relish the details of getting plans off the ground and using the skills of organizing and resourcing to make sure they stay airborne.

- *Recognize the gap between intention and impact.* Successfully eccentric leaders don't want to confuse people about what action is needed right now. They don't want people to think their leader is not serious about leading the company. They don't want to float scores of ideas without seeing at least some come to fruition.

Recognizing the gap between what they intend to do and what actually happens can jar eccentric leaders into making productive changes. Coaches are good at pointing out this gap by showing eccentrics results from feedback. Even if you're not being coached, however, you can identify this gap by charting your intentions and impact over a period of time. Note what you're trying to achieve and what you actually do achieve by talking to a trusted direct report. Go over your goals for the past year and ascertain if you've achieved them. Ask this direct report (or anyone in the company you feel will level with you) how your leadership style is perceived. Perhaps you view yourself as a highly creative leader who inspires and motivates through intellectual discourse and an "open" culture. Perhaps your people view you as a scattered and unfocused leader whose best ideas are wasted.

Typically, eccentric leaders flourish in creative, idea-oriented, constantly changing, and flexible environments—usually found in high-tech, research, marketing, entertainment, or image-driven company cultures. If you're working in one of these cultures, you may not have to act on these suggestions as quickly as someone in a more conservative environment—but the higher you are or the more people are depending on you for consistent behavior, the likelier it is that your eccentricity will become a potential derailer. Unclear priorities and the inability to execute will eventually doom any leader.

CHAPTER NINE

Passive Resistance

Your Silence Is Misinterpreted as Agreement

This derailer is more subtle than the others. CEOs who are passive-resistant may look to all the world like savvy leaders, people who know how to play politics and be pragmatic about goals. Underneath this surface, however, is unconscious duplicity. During meetings, such CEOs may nod in agreement and say they fully support a project, but privately they will talk about how dumb the project is and withhold real support. They create expectations among their people that they don't meet, confusing and disappointing them in the short term and creating cynicism in the long run.

Does this sound like you? If it does, you're probably saying to yourself, "Every successful executive in our organization behaves this way to a certain extent." It's true that we all play our cards close to the vest in politicized environments, not wishing to offend a sensitive coworker or unwilling to confront an influential boss. We may also assume a deliberately neutral pose, even though we know exactly how we're going to vote on an issue. Occasionally, it is wise, even important, to not fully disclose your position on a critical issue until others have weighed in.

A passive-resistant leader—one who is bound to fail—acts this way consistently and strategically. These behaviors are habitual, ingrained, and reflexive. It is almost as if the passive-resistant have two personalities, the private and public ones. Privately, they have their own agenda, and it often doesn't align with their public statements and actions.

Private agendas help people succeed in organizations up to a certain point. By creating the illusion of giving people what they want (support, resources, or whatever) and working the system to fulfill their own agendas, passive-resistant leaders can be seen as high-potential candidates for jobs. They are often quite adept at disguising the contradiction between their public and private personas, and so they seem like the sort of savvy, results-focused leaders that selection committees love. Being political and goal-oriented are valuable skills, but passive-resistant leaders do not use these skills in the best interests of the organization. Failure results because there's a jarring disconnect between the expectations they create and the realities they deliver.

A Culture Where No One Says What She Thinks

Anne was the founder and president of a catalog house that had significantly broadened its scope, acquiring two companies in the direct marketing field and establishing a partnership with a dot-com firm to help Anne's company market their products on the Web. Though it was a young organization, it was growing at a good rate and was well funded—a prominent venture capital firm had provided the seed money to start the company and was helping fund its expansion strategy.

Confident and ambitious, Anne was a good leader during the company's early growth period. Her people, though, were sometimes disconcerted by the way she'd say one thing and do another—she'd promised more than one of her direct reports a substantial raise that turned out to be not particularly substantial—but they made excuses for her, figuring she meant what she promised but circumstances prevented her from following through.

When sales leveled off, though, everyone noticed a greater discrepancy between Anne's words and actions. During meetings and in one-on-one conversations, Anne was bullish about the company's future, reassuring everyone that the growth strategy would be unaffected by slower sales. At the same time, though, she began a cost-cutting, downsizing process that surprised everyone. When one of her direct reports challenged her about this contradiction, Anne made a very persuasive argument that the company's future would be bright precisely because she was making sure she kept costs in line.

Anne's passive-resistant behaviors rubbed off on others. With its young, developing, and impressionable culture, the company mirrored the leadership style of its founder. Managers gave their people the impression that everything was going well while sending out their résumés when they heard of job openings elsewhere. When one of these managers would leave, team members would be angry that they had been deceived and soon became very cynical about the company in general—and specifically about Anne.

The venture capital people, too, were angry with Anne. She met regularly with her VC partner, and they'd go over the balance sheets and discuss the expansion strategy. During these meetings, he asked her to promise him that she'd move forward cautiously because of the recessionary economy and to consult the firm before making any major moves. She assured him she would do so. Nonetheless, she made a third major acquisition without consulting the firm. Anne confided to her CFO that she knew what was best for her company and that the venture capital firm would be grateful when the acquisition proved successful.

The venture capital people were not grateful, nor were they willing to wait and see how the acquisition turned out. They had witnessed Anne's passive-resistant behavior in the past, and this was the final straw. They demanded her resignation, threatening that they would withdraw the funding for the expansion strategy if she didn't comply. Reluctantly, she resigned, though she was convinced to the end that she had done nothing wrong.

Have You Crossed the Line?

If this is your big derailer, you're going to have to work hard to become aware of your derailing behaviors. We've found that passive-resistant leaders are very good at convincing themselves and others that their behavior is justified. They will justify the discrepancy between word and deed by insisting that political circumstances warrant the gap, or by maintaining that it was the wrong time and place to get into an argument about their real position.

All this may be true, but if you're consistently pretending to go along while privately going in another direction, then you've crossed the line. Look at the following delineations and see where you fall:

You say one thing and do another only when there's no other option.	Saying one thing and doing another is your standard operating procedure.
—————————————×—————————————	

People generally know what drives you.	You have a private agenda that you share with no one.
You try to avoid conflict but level with people when it's crucial they know where you're coming from.	You avoid conflict at all costs and rarely express any disagreement.
You have a sense of what other people expect of you and your commitments to them.	You don't know or care what others expect of you.

Signs and Symptoms

It's easy to justify passive-resistant behavior during difficult times. You may tell yourself that presidents during times of war can't tell the public everything—they don't want word to leak to the enemy or they don't want to cause unnecessary alarm—and so you too must do a bit of dissembling. To an extent, you are correct—all leaders, at times, must carefully decide how much of their private reservations or feelings to disclose. But you're probably passive-resistant if the following signs and symptoms regularly appear:

• *Confused and angry direct reports.* Do your direct reports frequently seem uncertain or ill-tempered? This is a common reaction to a passive-resistant leader. When their boss doesn't follow through on commitments, they're initially confused. When their boss continuously thwarts their expectations—especially expectations related to commitments, deliverables, promotions, compensation, or resource support—they become angry. If you're wondering why people are wary, indirect with you, or unwilling to believe your public commitments or sign up for your newest initiative—recognize it may be a sign of impending failure.

- *Rampant cynicism.* If confusion is the first stage, and anger the second, cynicism is the third and most alarming response to a passive-resistant leader. Listen for comments that suggest people distrust management, that indicate they don't believe promises will be kept. You may still have time to step back from the edge when confusion and anger are the predominant reactions, but cynicism means people have come to lack faith in your leadership—sometimes for very good reasons.

- *Alliances, teams, and partnerships that fall apart.* To the passive-resistant leader, the disintegration of a team or a partnership may seem to have clear causes. You may blame "personality conflicts" or "circumstances beyond your control." One passive-resistant CEO whose alliances regularly failed to deliver blamed both bad luck and "young rebels" for these outcomes and never acknowledged it might have something to do with the way he first raised expectations with his initial enthusiasm and then systematically undermined these expectations with his private complaints and criticisms, which he didn't discuss openly with his partners. Customers, strategic partners, and even vendors have a low tolerance for partnerships with passive-resistant people and will often terminate or exploit these partnerships.

- *Giving lip service.* You say you believe in certain things, but know as you're saying them that it's not the whole truth. "I believe we should be a people-oriented company" or "I want to always put the customer first" are two common sentiments that CEOs regularly extol, but in the back of their mind a little voice is whispering, "Not completely!" If you make these statements frequently because you're trying to meet the expectations of others and don't want your real views known, then it's a sign of this derailer.

Breaking Through Your Resistance

As we've noted, this derailer can be coaching-proof. You may automatically resist efforts to help you deal with the negative behaviors that come with a passive-resistant leadership style. Even as you're reading this, you may be creating a list of private opinions you have rationalized should not be shared openly in most contexts. For the following suggestions to be effective, you need to be open-minded about the possibility that your rationalizations are not only inaccurate but represent a trait that might cause you to fail. If it helps, keep in mind that if you become labeled as passive-resistant, it can be a career-killer. We've found that people who have reputations for saying one thing and doing another are eventually found out over time. No one completely trusts them, and a distrusted leader has difficulty finding both followers and top jobs today.

To prevent passive-resistant tendencies from derailing your career, try the following:

- *Understand the gap between how you're feeling and what you're saying or doing.* Force yourself to pay attention to this gap.

In meetings, presentations, and one-on-one discussions, decide if what you're communicating mirrors what you're thinking and feeling. It may help to review the results of 360-degree feedback. Passive-resistant leaders are usually surprised to discover how angry their people are because of this gap. Seeing the effect of their behaviors often catalyzes them to take positions more consistent with what they feel and believe.

• *Put yourself in the place of people you work with.* We tend to think that people are just like us, so if you're passive-resistant, you probably assume (unconsciously, perhaps) that everyone says one thing and does another, and the fact that you're doing it is no big deal. In reality, it is a big deal to other people. Therefore, put yourself in their place by gathering information from them about the following:

> What is the other person's expectation of you or what you and your group or organization will deliver?
> What commitments have you made? What commitment is this other individual counting on?
> Are you making an effort to align with these commitments and deliver on them?

• *Work on potential areas of conflict.* Your reluctance to engage in debate or express disagreement in certain settings may be causing you to mask your real feelings about issues. If you are able to make conflict explicit rather than keeping it inside yourself, you'll lessen the impact of this derailer. Think about the following and you should be more willing to communicate honestly when you disagree with someone or need to say no:

What are the most common issues (people, promotions, investment decisions, or whatever) where you're likely to be in
genuine disagreement with others?

What is the nature of the disagreement?

Why do you have difficulty being explicit about these areas?

• *Look to other successful leaders for models.* Passive-resistant
people benefit greatly from seeing that there are viable alterna-
tives to their own behaviors. This doesn't mean they have to radically alter their leadership style, but that they can be successful
even if they are more explicit about their thoughts and feelings
and don't work off of a private agenda. General Electric, for
example, evaluates leaders based on their consistency of message
across groups (analysts, employees, customers, and so on) and
downgrades those leaders who try to reserve one message for one
group and a different message for another.

Examine the Reason Behind Your Private Agenda

We want to make sure you don't jump to conclusions about this
derailer, since it's a subtle one in certain ways. Don't automatically assume that you possess this leadership flaw because you say
one thing and do another in certain situations. Being completely
honest and above board in all your leadership actions isn't just
rare—it's pathological. We're human, after all, and sometimes we
know that if we say exactly what we want to achieve, we may be
making a political or strategic blunder. You may know you need
to cut jobs in the next twelve months given the financial projections you just received from your CFO, but you decide not to create unnecessary alarm when you meet with employees until
you're certain what actions you intend to take. Though you sus-

pect it will be necessary, you can put off the decision for at least a few months, so your public stance is that you're considering all actions right now.

On the other hand, let's say you enthusiastically endorse expense control as a way to control costs and avoid layoffs, but privately you believe downsizing is inevitable because expense controls never yield sufficient results. Your public position is inconsistent with what you know and feel, but you do not want to be negative—so you tell your entire executive team as well as the Board and the media that you believe the financial results are improving. If you have convinced yourself that you are not really misleading anyone, you're just being positive and upbeat in order to lead effectively, you are probably passive-resistant.

The reason you consistently have private reservations you do not share is key. Is it to advance your career, manage the perceptions of others, protect yourself, or pursue a strategy that you know everyone else disagrees with? Or does it have to do with the welfare of the company and the people who work for it? Admittedly, this can be a fine line, but it's useful to consider the answer.

You should also consider how often there's a gap between your private and public agendas. There are going to be instances when your ego, your political savvy, or some other factor will cause you to say one thing and do another. If this happens only occasionally, passive resistance is probably not a derailer for you. It's only when this is standard operating procedure that you should be concerned.

We'd like to leave you with a final word of warning about this derailer: Passive-resistant behavior, while perhaps a part of the leadership repertoire in the big, slow-moving bureaucracies of the past, is quickly falling from favor. There's a trend toward transparency in organizations, and operating from a private agenda flies in the face of this trend. For CEOs especially, an implied psychological contract exists: You're here, you commit, and you align. You violate this contract when your deeds say, *I'm here but I'm not really here, I'm committed but not really committed, I'm aligned but not really aligned.*

CHAPTER TEN

Perfectionism

You Get the Little Things Right While the Big Things Go Wrong

I magine if Tony Randall were a CEO. More specifically, imagine him in the role of Felix Unger on the old television show, *The Odd Couple*, a role in which he played a finicky, detail-oriented man who went ballistic whenever he encountered a mess. As a CEO, Felix would be a disaster, especially when he was under stress. He would obsessively count every paper clip and quickly grow frustrated with any direct report who failed to do the job exactly as Felix envisioned. No doubt, his company would have the cleanest cafeteria and the most efficient processes, but it would also miss significant opportunities because of its unwavering focus on efficiency.

Perfectionistic CEOs often ignore the big picture. They're so wrapped up in the little things that they lose sight of all the major developments around them. Perfectionism is crucial for certain professions—doctors, accountants, aviators, engineers—and a small dose of it is useful for anyone in a position where mistakes can be literally or figuratively fatal. When this tendency causes a leader to lock in on the detail and lock out the real goal of the company or group, then it becomes a derailer.

At first glance, you may think that the perfectionistic class of leaders overlaps with the overly cautious one. It is true that both types may not be satisfied until they gather all the details, but the overly cautious CEOs are afraid of failure while the perfectionists are not. Instead, their irrational fears center on messy, chaotic situations that can't be neatly summed up. They are terrified of ambiguous choices that don't yield a clear decision after rigorous analysis.

An Irrational Need to Pick Nits

Making sure that all the i's are dotted and all the t's are crossed can be important leadership attributes. Many top CEOs have pushed themselves to be perfect, chastising themselves and their people when mistakes are made or a project isn't implemented with great care. Playing devil's advocate for a second, we might argue that this desire to do things perfectly can motivate leaders to work harder than others and avoid the silly mistakes that often doom otherwise promising initiatives. The devil indeed may be in the details, but we would advise you to take that adage two ways.

It may make sense to achieve perfection in areas of product safety, clinical trials, and manufacturing processes, but in countless other areas "good enough" really is good enough. When you try to be perfect about things that don't require perfection, that's when failure happens. Here are two examples that illustrate this point.

We coached John, a financial services company senior vice president, who'd been fired earlier in his career because of his perfectionistic traits. During the coaching process, John became increasingly aware of these traits and was remarkably articulate about them. This is John's description of his perfectionism and how it derailed his career:

> I was a straight A student all the way through graduate school, but I always fussed and fretted over every paper and

every test. It seemed to me my success in school was related to my impeccable preparation, so it was natural for me to use this same approach at work. I earned a reputation for catching mistakes and being willing to invest the time to make sure everything went smoothly on projects. This really helped me advance in my career.

As I was given more and more responsibility, there was more and more pressure. I couldn't stop thinking about how if I made a mistake, it could cost the company millions of dollars. Sometimes I had to make very difficult decisions, and it bothered me a lot that I couldn't control every aspect of these decisions. So I paid the most attention to what I could control. I'd rehearse my presentations for days to be sure they came off without a hitch or I'd triple-check the figures in my budget to make sure they weren't off. Probably the worst thing I did was refuse to give my direct reports much responsibility. I was convinced that none of them would pay as much attention to all aspects of a task as I did, so it made sense to me that I should handle it.

At my former company, I was so overworked that I became a drone. I realize now that I wasn't a very good manager and that I was spending far too much time on jobs my people could have handled, but I had somehow convinced myself that something awful would happen if I neglected all these minor matters. My boss told me I was let go because I wasn't developing my people and other groups complained that our group took forever to get something done.

It's still difficult for me to take a step back and recognize that perfection isn't always a virtue. It's a knee-jerk reaction, though, especially when a lot is riding on the outcome of my work. While it's tough to trust other people to handle some of the details, I realize I'm going to fail again if I don't stop fixating on every single task that comes in my direction.

Jill Barad, the former CEO of Mattel, wasn't as obsessively perfect as John, but she was known as extremely hands-on. When product options were presented to her, for example, she would dive down into the details of specific features—leaving her direct reports to define her as meddlesome. "It is a blatant problem," according to one former executive. "Why is the chairman looking at every design concept?" Barad was even known to snap at a secretary bringing her water: "This better not be tap!"

This type of attention to detail can be warranted in certain situations, but as a management style it creates unnecessary work for direct reports who may attempt to anticipate every possible reaction and question from the boss. We have worked with CEOs who spent hours picking out art for corporate anterooms, decreed curtains to be opened only to a certain width throughout headquarters, and even decided the menu in the executive dining room.

Have You Crossed the Line?

The line between being committed to doing the job right and perfectionism is often difficult to discern. Unlike some of the other derailers, this one can operate under the radar for a while without any serious negative consequences. People usually don't complain about perfectionists the way they do about arrogant and volatile leaders, for instance. For this reason, you may not think anything is amiss until your failure to see the big picture rears up and bites you.

Here are some ways to determine if your perfectionistic behaviors will ultimately result in failure:

You focus on the details.	Detail focus prevents you from seeing the bigger picture.
You find it worthwhile to make sure that presentations look and sound great.	You pay more attention to the form of presentations than to their substance.
You feel uncomfortable with uncertainty and ambiguity.	You try to impose structure in every situation to get rid of uncertainty and ambiguity.
You manage processes with skill and determination.	You spend so much time managing processes that people's needs become secondary.
You are conscientious about your responsibilities.	You can't let go of any task no matter how small until it's completed exactly as you had wanted.

Signs and Symptoms

Perfectionists are often fastidious. We've known executives with this derailer who obsessed over last quarter's numbers, or who insisted that their team follow a certain procedure or policy to the letter even when it was obvious to everyone that it didn't make sense to follow it so rigidly. These perfectionistic behaviors spring from good impulses—they are taking responsibility for doing the job right—but they become warped when people don't differentiate between jobs and manage these impulses. If you want to find a perfectionistic leader, look for the one who seems focused on details but can't seem to spot trends or macro changes in the marketplace. Here are some other signs and symptoms:

- *Difficulty delegating.* This is the most obvious symptom of this derailer, though it may also be a symptom of other derailers. You can determine if the problem is perfectionism by examining the why behind this symptom. Perfectionists shy away from delegating because they want to be absolutely sure others do the job as perfectly as they would do it themselves. They think: "Bob won't be as diligent about it as I would be; Stephanie won't examine the situation from all angles; Tom won't double-check the figures he gets from Joan like I would. It is up to me."

- *Putting form over function, style over substance.* It's not that you believe that it's more important to have a good-looking report cover than a good report. But you may spend an inordinate amount of time on secondary tasks, convincing yourself that "the little things add up to a big thing." When CEOs are caught up in matters of form and style, they come across as superficial. They have the mandate and the power to change organizations, and instead they concentrate on changing the company's vacation policy. Because CEOs must deal with long-range issues, time frames, and outcomes, sometimes it is satisfying to focus on the chair arrangements for the analyst meeting, the décor of the company plane, or the color scheme of the annual report. But if issues like these become common preoccupations, derailment is a distinct possibility.

• *Shortchanging people.* When process engineering was popular a number of years ago, many companies focused on process mapping and reengineering. When reengineering as a trend began to peak, many leaders made the wise observation, "We were so busy reengineering processes, we forgot about the people." Some perfectionistic leaders remain enmeshed in the process; they spend inordinate amounts of time and energy on Six Sigma, human resources policies, and other mechanical issues. There's nothing inherently wrong in being a process person, but it's a sign of impending failure when it takes away from a leader's ability to connect with people on what's important. People are a lot messier than processes, and it's easier to redesign a flawed process than it is to deal with a flawed direct report. If you're retreating from people and finding solace in processes, then it's a sign that this may be your derailer.

• *Overlooking the obvious.* If you regularly say to yourself, "How could I have missed that?" it may indicate perfectionistic tendencies. When you're obsessed with the details, you miss trends and changes that can affect your business. Paying attention to subtle changes in the market—from the emergence of new global players to e-commerce innovations to new technologies—and responding to them with appropriate strategies is what leadership is all about. CEOs who overlook these big picture shifts or don't pay attention when their direct reports communicate them may be perfectionists.

• *Getting caught in the vicious stress cycle.* When leaders fail because of their perfectionist impulses, they often do so because they're trapped in this stress cycle. Things start going downhill, and they respond by trying to do everything even more perfectly than they did in the past, hoping this will relieve the stress. In fact, this action ratchets up the stress because trying to be perfect is incredibly difficult, if not impossible. If you find yourself getting caught in this cycle, then this may be a derailer you need to watch out for.

Perfection Is an Ideal: How to Deal with the Reality

Perfectionists often are aware of their tendencies. Less denial exists around this derailer than many of the others. Nonetheless, people are all too quick to rationalize their perfectionistic behaviors. If you call a leader of this type perfectionistic, odds are the reply will be a satisfied nod and a quiet, "Yes, I'm tremendously demanding of myself and others," or, "Others just don't care as much as I do."

Being demanding is fine. Being detailed to the point of obsession is not. Here are some ways you can prevent perfectionism from derailing your career:

• *Examine the costs.* You're never going to back off your perfectionistic behaviors until you recognize the negative impact it's having on your career and your company. If you think the costs are that it takes you longer to get something done because you need to check all the details, you're seriously underestimating the toll these behaviors take. To assess the true costs, look at the following list and ask yourself if you're paying these prices:

Stressed out. Do you feel exhausted every day at work? Does it seem like it's impossible to do all the tasks you've set for yourself? Are you having trouble sleeping? Do you find yourself getting little joy out of what you do, but doing it more than ever before? These are all signs of the overstressed leader, and eventually they will catch up with you. Personally, you may simply blow up or shut down if you keep pursuing the impossible pipe dream of perfection. Professionally, you're bound to make mistakes because your judgment is clouded by your self-imposed stress.

Missed opportunities. Does it seem as if you're overlooking important facts when making decisions or that other companies or leaders are faster to move on opportunities than you are? Does the competition bring to market products or ideas you have been relentlessly researching? Do you feel like events take you by surprise even though others say they were predictable? Are you missing chances to grow your company or capitalize on your group's strengths because you're so busy correcting mistakes and double-checking other people's work? Is the cost of a missed opportunity worth having all the little things completed to your satisfaction?

Diminished productivity from direct reports. Your people can't be productive if you don't delegate. Think about how many times you've chosen to withhold assignments from direct reports because you were convinced you would do it right and they wouldn't. Assess what your people are actually working on and if the majority of their assignments are significant or minor; if the latter, why aren't they working on meatier projects? If you do give them a significant project, what do you value most in their work? Is it matters of form such as how a report looks and if they've followed procedure to the letter? Do you find yourself regularly "drilling down" in presentations to a level of detail no one can answer—or needs to?

• *Prioritize the key jobs and learn to live with imperfection on less important projects.* Prioritizing is tough for perfectionists because in their minds everything is critical. Force yourself to select three to five assignments that must be done right, and apply your detail-minded approach to them. At the same time, relax your standards with the others. CEOs especially need to learn to live with inadequate performance from others at times. If they demand superior work from everyone all the time, they will become disappointed, frustrated, and stressed. You can stop perfectionism from being a derailer if you accept imperfection in appropriate circumstances.

• *Give up a perfectionistic behavior.* We've saved the toughest assignment for last. To facilitate giving up this behavior, start out by writing how you typically behave in a given work situation that results in one of the costs just discussed. Maybe you're describing how your obsessiveness about matters of form and style put you under tremendous stress. Perhaps you focus on how you hoard important assignments because you fear your direct reports will mess them up. As you write about the experience, specify how you, your group, or your organization suffered as a result. Then rewrite the situation, choosing to give up a perfectionistic behavior. In one new scenario, you might decide to give up an important project and allow a direct report to take over. Or you might give up a certain amount of detail work, deciding that ignoring it won't cause any major problems. Rehearsing giving up a behavior on paper makes giving it up in real life a little bit easier.

CHAPTER ELEVEN

Eagerness to Please

You Want to Win Any Popularity Contest

P eople please CEOs and not the other way around, or at least that's the common conception. It's assumed that CEOs have so much power that they don't worry about what other people think or how to meet other people's needs.

In fact, we've known many CEOs who were extremely eager to please, and they've reached this capstone position precisely because they're skilled at anticipating and meeting expectations. Typically, these pleasers are highly astute at figuring out what other people want. They're not spineless followers; they possess a keen political sense and have an uncanny knack of delivering the right resources, information, and ideas to the right people at the right time. Their ability to achieve consensus is well known, and they derive great satisfaction from serving the organization as a whole and all the individual employees in it.

Pleasers can be enormously popular because of these qualities, but they can also fail because of them. Their aversion to conflict and contentious debate causes them to bury contrary opinions that need to be heard. When CEOs are pleasers, they fail in part because their companies have access only to the conventional wisdom. The unconventional wisdom—where innovation and bold moves originate—is largely absent.

Bending Over Backward to Please—and Then Failing

Carl is the CEO of a company in the food industry that was dominated by veteran senior managers. Carl was immediately tagged a high-potential when he joined the company and quickly moved up because of his expertise and his knack for "delivering the goods," as one of his coworkers put it. Carl invested a lot of energy and effort in figuring out what his bosses expected of him. He'd ask questions of them and others until he was sure he understood what was required and then he worked hard to meet these requirements. Contrary to what you might think, Carl wasn't a sycophant. He didn't excessively flatter his bosses or say what they wanted to hear. Instead, Carl worked harder and more intelligently than most to meet other people's objectives. He was also politically savvy and managed to get himself assigned to teams and groups that had high-visibility projects. People noticed Carl, and as he was promoted from one position to the next, it seemed that he could do no wrong.

When Carl was named CEO, it was a popular choice. Carl was viewed as a genuinely good person who was also very smart about the business—it seemed like a perfect selection. But within the first six months of his tenure, Carl started to struggle. Carl had inherited a senior vice president, Dan, whose performance was going downhill rapidly. Dan ignored meetings, failed to deliver projects on time, and generally acted as if he were invulnerable. Carl knew he had to confront him, but he procrastinated. He knew Dan had a bad temper, and he was sure he'd be furious no matter what he said.

Finally, he summoned the nerve to meet with him, told him it wasn't working out, and Dan quickly became angry and challenging. He demanded a compensation package far in excess of what he deserved (and more than the company had ever given anyone), but Carl caved in to his demands. He rationalized his decision by telling his team that Dan had served the company well for ten years and deserved to be treated "with respect" for that service. He said that they shouldn't punish him for his apathy and attitude of the past year.

As you might expect, Carl's people were incredulous. They couldn't believe he didn't stand up to Dan since he didn't deserve half of the package the company gave him. The episode with Dan set a dangerous precedent. A few other people took advantage of Carl, knowing that all it took for them to get what they wanted was to throw a fit. Other members of the senior management group were confused by Carl's decisions; he wasn't assigning resources based on which groups or opportunities deserved them but on who made the biggest fuss. As a result, many members of the executive committee became frustrated, even though Carl tried to placate them. He spent so much time smoothing ruffled feathers and investing in the wrong projects that the company had a difficult year.

Carl, recognizing that eagerness to please was his derailer, has been working on managing it and remains CEO. Still, the company has suffered because of his unconscious desire to make everyone happy, and his career has also suffered. Though Carl is still a very well-liked CEO, he is seen by some board members as "not strong enough," and no doubt some of them have come to the unfortunate conclusion that he may have difficulty being "tough enough" to run this company.

Have You Crossed the Line?

We're not advocating that all CEOs become tough SOBs. There's plenty of middle ground. Ideally, leaders will know when to please and when not to. Or to put it slightly differently, they'll know how and when to satisfy the requirements of key people but also make wise choices as to whose requirements they'll satisfy.

Are you a pleaser? If you are, you probably answered this question by saying to yourself, "No, but I've got great people skills." That's probably true. These people skills, however, can be used to keep everyone as happy as possible rather than as productive as possible.

See if you've crossed the line and made yourself vulnerable to this derailer:

You believe that happy workers are good workers.	You believe that one unhappy worker can spoil the whole company.
The teams you create get things done through consensus.	The teams you create quickly snuff dissenting or anxiety-raising ideas.
You're able to adapt to new events and circumstances.	You're so flexible that no one (including you) is sure where you stand on issues.
You confront with compassion.	You confront without backbone.

You like to keep disagreements from disrupting meetings and the flow of work.	You communicate that disagreement and conflict are frowned upon, to the point that strong emotions are rarely expressed.

×

Signs and Symptoms

Early in your career, pleaser traits may have few or even no negative side effects. To all the world, you may appear to be someone who works well in all sorts of situations with all sorts of people, and your bosses think you're terrific. It's only as you gain increasing amounts of responsibility and supervise more people that failure happens. The higher your position in a company, the more stress you'll have because of this trait. It's tremendously difficult to satisfy everyone who works for you, especially when you're running a division or a department. CEOs typically have a group of direct reports with strong egos and confident demeanors who are often in conflict, usually exacerbated by scarce resources, matrix responsibilities, and interest in succession. Attempting to suppress conflict requires more energy than resolving it.

A pleaser's self-destructive behaviors often emerge in uncertain environments. For instance, a major customer may be on the verge of pulling out and switching suppliers. Or there may be sudden product liability issues that are not easily resolved. Or a competitor has chosen to lower prices significantly—setting off a price war that threatens profit projections for the year. This is when you're most likely to do what satisfies the majority rather than what you believe is the right course of action.

Given all this, recognize that the following signs and symptoms of pleaser-caused failure are more likely to emerge during stressful times when it's not clear what path should be pursued:

• *Losing people's support and loyalty.* The irony of being a pleaser is that you ultimately don't end up pleasing the majority of people. Pleasers try to promise everyone something, but these promises often can't be kept because one promise negates another. We worked with a CEO pleaser who reflexively cut deals with everyone who came into his office, but the only deal that would stick was the last one he cut because the next person in line would convince him to change his mind about something he'd just agreed upon. Therefore, a common strategy became to have the last appointment of the day or to see him just before he left on a trip or vacation.

While this last person might have been pleased with the deal, everyone else was not, and the company was beset with strong fiefdoms, silo behavior, and little teamwork. Pleasers lose support because direct reports see through them. They're not sincerely interested in helping an individual grow and succeed—all they want is to avoid unpleasantness. Promising one thing to please Direct Report A and then amending or negating that promise after cutting a deal with Direct Report B causes people to lose respect, regardless of the pleaser's role or position.

• *Unwillingness to stand up for your people.* This feeds into the previous symptom of losing support and loyalty. You may be a leader who caves in when customers insist that they don't want a specific sales executive working their account. You know your sales executive is implementing your agreed-upon strategy even though the customers don't like it, but you don't defend him when the customers raise objections about his performance. Or when a high-potential professional comes to you and complains that one of your direct reports is not a good leader—even though the alleged leadership infractions are a result of your request— you calm her down by apologizing for this direct report's blunder and saying you'll do something about it.

A team will fall apart when its senior leader refuses to support them publicly and privately. Not only will morale suffer, people will feel like it's futile to take strong positions because they assume their boss won't support them.

• *A lack of "fire" in the environment.* In their quest for peace and harmony, pleasers inadvertently rob their companies of creative tension. They are so fixated on keeping everyone at peace that they send the implicit message that conflict is taboo. In meetings, people talk calmly and rationally, without much emotion in their positions. In one-on-one discussions, they all avoid making their position "personal"—they don't make a passionate pitch about why they believe a given approach is right. As a result, these companies lack the combustible debates that energize teams and give rise to new ideas. While no one wants an environment where knock-down, drag-out arguments are the norm, the opposite is just as harmful to an organization.

• *Refusal to face the tough people decisions.* We've saved the most prominent symptom for last, in part because we've already alluded to it. Difficult decisions regarding people are the central requirement of the CEO role. All senior leaders find these decisions difficult, but pleasers find them especially challenging when they involve good people who are not producing. They hate removing someone who has been loyal to them or with whom they've worked for years. They resist having to pick one of two good people for a key job. They don't like being asked to referee a contentious debate between direct reports. When faced with these decisions, they may postpone them indefinitely or find some compromise position that allows them to avoid making a clear-cut choice. The negative consequences include carrying underperforming people and alienating direct reports who deserve promotions or the most important projects (and don't receive them).

A Reason to Believe:
Becoming Aware of What You Stand for

As executive coaches, we find pleasers both easy and difficult to work with. They're easy to work with because they want to please us as much as everyone else, so they're very accommodating when we make suggestions about how they might change. They often say something to the effect of, "I understand what you're telling me," or even, "that's an excellent suggestion!" They're difficult to deal with because they don't translate understanding into action. They would rather see us happy than commit to improve themselves or resist our coaching. We aren't always sure we're getting through to them. They respond as if we are, but nothing happens.

If eagerness to please is your derailer, here's what you can do to avoid failure by making something happen:

• *Identify what you believe.* Carl (from our earlier example) didn't know what he believed in. Without a clear sense of his business, management, and leadership philosophy, he lacked a leadership agenda and point of view. He was vulnerable to his desire to please. It's difficult to engage in conflict and make tough people decisions when you don't know where you stand on issues, and why your vision and values are as important as any one individual's resistance. It's a lot easier to tolerate an individual's anger or dissent if you have developed a strong point of view to reinforce your decisions. Without well-articulated beliefs, people seek the safe harbor of calm and consensus.

To avoid this illusory safe harbor, think about what you believe in terms of:

How work gets done

What work values you subscribe to

What behaviors should be rewarded

What you will and won't tolerate

The type of business strategy you believe is effective

Create a belief statement of a few sentences and refer to it when facing tough people decisions or before confronting individuals who need to be confronted.

• *Pick a fight.* In other words, force yourself to engage in conflict, even if it's a small-scale conflict. Of course, you don't want to do this arbitrarily or start bullying the first person you encounter. Instead, think about a situation where you might be more forceful or identify a conflict you're avoiding. Think about the positions you're not taking or the words you're not saying. Ask yourself if there are real risks in confronting an underperforming direct report or speaking forthrightly to a combative board. What is the worst thing another individual might do or say? Concentrate on how and why you're not confronting some-one; put the focus on you rather than on the person you're trying to satisfy or placate.

This exercise will help you take small steps away from pleasing everyone all the time. It will let you see that when you lack a 100 percent pleased populace, the business doesn't come to a grind-ing halt.

- *Defend someone who is worth defending.* Your consultant is insisting you get rid of your CFO. Your team is scapegoating a particular individual for a project's demise. Your board is resist-ing your choice of a successor. If you think the attackers are wrong, stand your ground and make your case. It may result in an argument; harsh words may be exchanged. But it's a great feel-ing to stand up for an individual (or a group) that you feel is in the right and has been wronged. It's a much better feeling than remaining silent. Becoming accustomed to that good feeling will make you less likely to want to please all the time.

The Irony of Making People Happy

If there is a cautionary tale to be told, it involves CEO Aaron Feuerstein of Malden Mills, the manufacturer of Polartec and a company that employed three thousand people. After a fire destroyed the factory, Feuerstein declared that he would rebuild it and spare no expense to ensure that it was a state-of-the-art place to work. As a result, he spent significantly more than his insurance covered. In addition, he paid his employees' salaries and benefits while they were off work and the new factory was being built.

Hailed as a hero, Feuerstein went far beyond what most other CEOs would have done. A few years later, Feuerstein filed for Chapter 11 protection.

The line between compassion and pleaser behavior is thin. Feuerstein did a wonderful thing in providing for his people in a difficult time. However, his company eventually had to lay off many people as debt increased, and it was down to many fewer employees at the Chapter 11 filing.

Were the people who were laid off pleased? While they might have considered their boss a hero initially, they probably were not so generous in their assessments later on. Feuerstein's actions are still debatable, but in hindsight, it seems as if his interest in the affection and admiration of his employees might have clouded his business judgment. If he had invested only the money allowed by his insurance policy to rebuild the factory and if he had offered reduced pay and incentives to sustain people while he rebuilt market share, he might have avoided bankruptcy. In the long run, it seems likely that his employees would have been more pleased if he had been less generous.

If eagerness to please is your derailer, factor common sense and real-world analysis into the equation before trying to make everyone happy. And recognize and remember the first rule of being a true leader: it is always better to be respected than liked.

CHAPTER TWELVE

Why CEOs Succeed

W hatever your derailers might be or however many you might have, you're much better off now that you're aware of them. We know that after having read about how each of these traits caused leaders to fail, you may fear that a derailer is like a time bomb ticking away inside of you just waiting for the right moment to ruin your career.

Of course, it's natural and appropriate to be concerned about those aspects of your personality that can inhibit your success; recognize that you now possess the knowledge necessary to manage them. Derailers do their damage when you're unaware of their existence. Many of the stories we've related in these pages concern leaders who were unaware. We have not told you, however, about a CEO we coach who has all eleven derailers but has never failed. In fact, he is one of the most successful and best-known CEOs in the world, and his commitment to managing his derailers—and the skills he has learned in doing so—have prevented his negative personality traits from doing him or his company any harm.

We would be the first to acknowledge that managing your derailers is easier when you have a coach to help you. But you can do it without a coach if you use the diagnostic and prescriptive tools provided in each chapter. To facilitate this self-coaching, we'd like to offer you a few additional suggestions.

What Kind of Stress Triggers Your Derailers?

What kind of environments, events, problems, and decisions ratchet your stress levels up to the nth degree? In what situations do you find yourself popping antacid tablets or wishing you hadn't given up smoking ten years ago? Some CEOs we've worked with have told us they feel the most stress when they have to make big decisions and there's no clear choice. Other CEOs have told us about the pressure of cutting employment, selling a favored business, firing a loyal but nonperforming executive, or some other action that they found necessary but difficult. Still others note that they're under the greatest stress when not much is happening—lack of action, even on vacation—makes them uncomfortable.

When stress rises, derailers are most likely to throw people off course. Being aware of the type of stress that you're particularly sensitive to will help you be alert for the derailer-caused behaviors that can catalyze failure. Review the following list and place a check mark next to those factors that trigger your stress response:

❑ Interactions with bosses, boards, big customers, or authority figures

❑ Major career or life transitions

❑ Mergers and acquisitions

❑ Failure of a program, team, or policy for which you are accountable

❑ Downsizing or restructuring

❑ Boredom

- ❏ Too much work
- ❏ Intense peer competition
- ❏ Deadlines
- ❏ Personal financial pressure
- ❏ Negative publicity
- ❏ Conflict
- ❏ Confronting underperforming direct reports
- ❏ Working in a matrix
- ❏ Dealing with paradox, complexity, uncertainty, or conflicting expectations
- ❏ Appeasing difficult customers

There's some overlap between these factors and we haven't covered every event or subject that could induce stress, but you'll probably find at least one that applies to you. Feel free to make this list more specific or add factors. You should also be aware of the more general factors that frequently place great pressure on leaders. Organizational change, for instance, often triggers derailers. So too do unrealistic expectations. Many CEOs complain that boards, analysts, employees, and the media look to them as saviors because of their position when, in fact, a CEO is highly dependent on others for success. These expectations add crushing pressure to an already high-pressure job.

In a larger sense, organizational environments are becoming increasingly demanding and stressful. The drive for results, currency fluctuations, regulatory pressures, economic uncertainty, leadership shortages, revenue and profit targets, demanding customers, and leading through influence rather than by positional authority all contribute to the stress leaders feel. Becoming aware of when, where, and how you feel stress won't eliminate the cause, but will allow you to be alert for your derailers in action.

Coaching Techniques: How to Use Your Inner and Outer Resources to Fight Failure

To supplement the techniques described in each chapter, you can do a number of things to understand what your derailers are and learn to manage them on your own. When coaching leaders, we often use these techniques, in addition to the CDR International Derailment Report, to help them confirm their suspicions about which derailers apply to them as well as to gather data that makes their diagnosis more specific. See if the following helps you:

• *Adversity analysis.* Close your office door, shut off the phone and computer, and think long and hard about the five biggest failures in your career. Write down the event and the outcome. Take your time and reflect on the disappointments and defeats that make up this list. When you've come up with five failures, ask yourself the following questions:

What behaviors in these circumstances didn't serve you well?

What would your worst critics say about how you acted?

Do you see a theme or pattern in your behaviors?

Do any of the derailers fit this pattern?

Most people don't do adversity analysis. Why would they? Who likes to dwell on their "stupidest" moves and biggest disappointments, especially when leaders are expected to be optimistic, confident, and upbeat? Yet looking at your career and yourself realistically is clearly the best window to understanding your derailers. If you have been removed from a key assignment, was it because you were too proud to admit you were wrong (arrogance)? Or was it because your nitpicking deflected your attention from the big picture (perfectionistic)? Are there clear and consistent patterns in your failures that deep inside yourself you know you had some role in creating?

• *Direct report evaluation.* Instead of locking yourself in an office, lock up your direct reports. Tell them you're going to leave them alone, and ask them to report back to you with their best ideas and recommendations after discussing the following question:

How can I be a better leader?

Make sure they understand that you want—that you expect—them to be brutally honest. Then clear out. What you'll discover is that your direct reports are acutely aware of your derailers, even if you aren't. Your derailers are their reality—and every day they may be complaining to each other about how smooth but indirect you can be, or how you just can't pull the trigger on important decisions. It probably seems to you as if your derailers are hidden from view, maybe even from yourself, but anyone who has worked with you over a sustained period has a good sense of your flaws—they often have to work around them. (If you doubt this, think back to some of the people you've worked for in the past. Did they display what you now recognize as symptoms of derailers? Do you think your direct reports are less perceptive than you were? If so, which derailer is that?) In fact, you might want to have your team answer the following supplemental questions:

What do I do that makes you nuts?
How do I force you to work around me rather than with me?

When you get together to complain about me, what do you
complain about?

When I'm under stress, what do I do that you think is counter-
productive?

You need to reassure your direct reports that nothing they say
will be held against them, and you have to focus on their collec-
tive opinion rather than who said what. You must keep this
promise or risk losing all credibility in their eyes and any possibility of feedback in the future. If they're honest with you, they'll
tip you off to which derailers you're vulnerable to.

• *Find a confidant.* A confidant is someone you can trust,
who understands your business context and who can provide you
with objective, insightful advice and feedback. Friends or spouses
have difficulty filling this role because they generally don't grasp
your business issues, and it's also difficult for them to be objective. Many people confuse confidants with organizational allies,
and this can be a painful mistake, since today's allies can become
tomorrow's competitors for resources, promotions, and people.

A mentor, retired or still active, might be a good choice. Someone who has observed you move up the organization, and knows
you better than anyone might be a possibility. You may trust
someone in human resources who has experience as a coach. A
former direct report whom you respect and trust might qualify.

This choice is not to be taken lightly. For a confidant to be
effective in helping you manage your derailers, you're going to
have to reveal some of your vulnerabilities. It's scary psychologically and it's scary from a career standpoint. The wrong person
can do you more harm than good. Therefore, assess your candidates carefully. Once you've made your choice, you should

provide your confidant with a list of the eleven derailers to provide a framework as they help you monitor your behavior. While talking with this confidant won't give you access to the same tools and techniques as talking with an executive coach, it will enable you to maintain a higher awareness level about the traits that may cause you to fail.

Finally, recognize that you might be reluctant to choose someone to be a confidant. CEOs sometimes experience the same hesitancy. We've worked with a number of CEOs who in our initial meetings seemed trained to not open themselves up very much to another individual. They have learned that admitting their vulnerabilities can be dangerous, or can violate the expectations of those who expect them to be strong and decisive. They're often convinced that no one can grasp the demands of their role unless it is another CEO, and that another individual could not help them confront the personal challenges they face. However, we have found that after working with us, they learn that derailers can be an easy tool and language to help them identify and manage their negative personality factors, and they often become great advocates for coaching. Still, it takes a leap of faith for any CEO to bring in a coach, and it may require a leap of faith for you to choose a confidant.

Why Companies Fail:
Addressing Organizational Leadership Derailers

As we've emphasized throughout this book, managing derailers helps both careers and companies. When a CEO and executive committee become aware of the traits that can trip them up and learn to discuss them openly, the entire company will benefit. They make better decisions because those decisions aren't made based on unconscious impulses. They accomplish more because they're not wasting energy in unproductive and tangential discussions. Most important, they can extend acceptance to each other and build a team based on trust and accountability—because they recognize and accept that all the team members are flawed but valuable human beings working to manage their negative impulses.

With their derailers under control, leaders free up their strengths. They're less engaged in acting out, hiding behind, or pretending. As a group, they more likely to focus their attention on business success factors rather than personal agendas. Leaders who acknowledge their derailers do not minimize their individual styles or personalities or gravitate toward some bland organizational mean. You're still going to have executives who are perfectionists, pleasers, and the like. But when they manage their derailers, they can survive handily—the dangerous traits don't diminish their effectiveness.

We've found that when we coach a leadership group, it has a trickle-down effect to the entire company. At Bank of America, for instance, we coached more than fifteen hundred of the most senior executives on their derailment factors in a series of workshops during a two-year period. Bank of America executives became very public about their derailers with each other and their teams. They routinely talked about how their derailers have a negative impact on others and on their own ability to be successful, and could even joke with each other about those moments when their derailment factors were taking over.

Companies willing to address the issue of individual leadership derailment as an organizational issue can improve performance by examining and improving their leadership talent pool.

For instance, they may ask: What does it mean for our company if our executive leadership is top-heavy with overly cautious people? How does this impede our ability to take risks, move quickly, and be decisive? At Avon Products we looked at the derailers of the top five hundred executives and identified issues that were likely to get in the way of successfully executing their strategy. These insights helped them determine what actions were necessary for the company to manage its organizational derailers and meet the expectations of all its stakeholders. Increasingly, companies want us to coach a group of senior executives in order to create a critical mass of people who have learned to manage their derailers. They recognize that if their top people are open and honest about their flaws, they will help create a culture of openness and honesty. We recently worked with one company whose Executive Committee was filled with pleasers. They were acutely aware of their inability to take strong public positions, risk alienating customers, or even confront each other. Once they understood their team profile they began to challenge each other and the company began to change.

Understanding and managing leadership derailers doesn't just create better leaders, it creates better followers. All direct reports sometimes perceive their bosses in a less-than-positive light. They may see them as mean-spirited, manipulative, intolerant, inattentive, or even worse. In fact, these negative traits only come out when bosses are under stress and aren't aware of their derailers. When direct reports realize that the behavior is an aspect of the boss's personality rather than the entire individual, they can be less defensive. They can understand that they are seeing a boss at his worst in particular circumstances rather than how he really is—they become more tolerant of these negative behaviors. In many instances, they provide their bosses with the type of feedback that help them get control of their negative actions.

Companies frequently experience serious setbacks when entire groups of people collude to overlook, deny, or manage around a CEO's negative personality characteristics. We have witnessed the demise of once great companies such as Enron, Kmart, Global Crossing, Tyco, and others—realizing far too late that one factor in their failure was the fact that no one could tell the emperor the truth. When CEOs, senior executives, and especially boards of directors become familiar with derailers—and hold each other accountable for managing them—there is less likelihood that unfortunate events will occur.

An Evolved View of Leadership

Central to this discussion of leadership derailment is the fact that leaders aren't perfect. Whether you're a CEO or senior executive, you know the constant, crushing pressure of unrealistic expectations. Part of this is self-imposed, but part of it comes from other sources: the media, competitors, customers, boards of directors, and employees. In the past, CEOs went to great lengths to hide their weaknesses, and they were able to do so. They were often able to shield from public view their less-than-flattering behaviors as well as their less-than-flattering personalities. They could decide what to communicate, how, and when. In a less demanding time and a less transparent society, they could create the illusion of perfection.

That's no longer possible today, and society's view of leadership needs to evolve accordingly. As long as leaders try to be perfect and expect perfection, they're going to be more vulnerable to our derailers. They're going to be especially vulnerable as pressure for improved performance intensifies, as global competition and uncertainty increases, and as the Internet and other technological innovations continue to change traditional ways of doing business. Although many leaders we know fantasize about "the time when things will return to normal," as far as we can tell, derailer-triggering stress isn't going to go away any time soon.

To deal effectively with stress, the first step is to accept that you—that all leaders—are fallible. Although many corporations do not acknowledge it, their entire leadership ranks are made up of flawed human beings. What needs to be more openly acknowledged is that flawed human beings can still be great leaders.

Accepting this will free you to become aware of your derailers—and, rather than to deny or minimize them, to learn to manage them. Increased stress may be inevitable, but failure is not. Chief executives and senior leaders do not have to become objects of derision because of dumb mistakes and insulated arrogance that get them and their companies into difficulty. Instead, they can make headlines with astute moves that drive their companies to superior performance. *Why CEOs Succeed* is a book we'd like to write, but it's only going to be written when more leaders learn to manage their derailers.

PROFESSIONAL LITERATURE

Badaracco, J. L., Jr. *Defining Moments: Choosing Between Right and Right.* Boston: Harvard Business School Press, 1997.

Badaracco, J. L., Jr. "We Don't Need Another Hero." *Harvard Business Review,* Sept. 2001, pp. 120–126.

Badaracco, J. L., Jr. *Leading Quietly: An Unorthodox Guide to Doing the Right Thing.* Boston: Harvard Business School Press, 2002.

Badaracco, J. L., Jr., and Ellsworth, R. R. *Leadership and the Quest for Integrity.* Boston: Harvard Business School Press, 1993.

Block, P. *Stewardship: Choosing Service Over Self-Interest.* San Francisco: Berrett-Koehler, 1996.

Boehm, C. *Hierarchy in the Forest.* Cambridge, Mass.: Harvard University Press, 1999.

Bossidy, L., and Charan, R. *Execution: The Discipline of Getting Things Done.* New York: Crown, 2002

Burns, J. M. *Leadership.* New York: Harper & Row, 1978.

Charan, R. *What the CEO Wants You to Know: How Your Company Really Works.* New York: Crown, 2001.

Charan, R., and Colvin, G. "Why CEOs Fail." *Fortune,* June 21, 1999, p. 69.

Collins, J. *Good to Great: Why Some Companies Make the Leap . . . and Others Don't.* New York: HarperCollins, 2001.

Conger, J. A. *Spirit at Work: Discovering the Spirituality in Leadership.* San Francisco: Jossey-Bass, 1994.

Cooper, R. K., and Sawaf, A. *Executive EQ: Emotional Intelligence in Leadership and Organizations.* New York: Putnam, 1997.

Dotlich, D. L., and Cairo, P. C. *Action Coaching: How to Leverage Individual Performance for Company Success.* San Francisco: Jossey-Bass, 2001.

Dotlich, D. L., and Cairo, P. C. *Unnatural Leadership: Ten New Leadership Instincts.* San Francisco: Jossey-Bass, 2002.

Dotlich, D. L., and Noel, J. L. *Action Learning: How the World's Top Companies are Re-Creating Their Leaders and Themselves.* San Francisco: Jossey-Bass, 1998.

Edler, R. *If I Knew What I Know Now: CEOs and Other Smart Executives Share Wisdom They Wish They'd Been Told 25 Years Ago.* New York: Berkley, 1997.

Egan, G. *Working the Shadow Side: A Guide to Positive Behind-the-Scenes Management.* San Francisco: Jossey-Bass, 1994.

Foster, R., and Kaplan, S. *Creative Destruction: Why Companies That Are Built to Last Underperform the Market—and How to Successfully Transform Them.* New York: Doubleday, 2001.

Fox, J. J. *How to Become CEO: The Rules for Rising to the Top of Any Organization.* New York: Hyperion, 1998.

Fuller, J. "A Letter to the Chief Executive." *Harvard Business Review,* Oct. 2002, pp. 94–99.

Goleman, D. *Emotional Intelligence.* New York: Bantam Books, 1997.

Goleman, D. *Working with Emotional Intelligence.* New York: Bantam Books, 1998.

Handy, C. *The Hungry Spirit: Beyond Capitalism: A Quest for Purpose in the Modern World.* New York: Broadway Books, 1999.

Hathaway, S. R., and McKinley, J. C. *Manual for the Minnesota Multiphasic Personality Inventory.* New York: Psychological Corporation, 1943.

Heifetz, R. *Leading Without Easy Answers.* Cambridge, Mass.: Belknap Press, 1994.

Heifetz, R., and Linsky, M. *Leadership on the Line: Staying Alive Through the Dangers of Leading.* Boston: Harvard Business School Press, 2002.

Hogan, R., and Hogan, J. "Assessing Leadership: A View from the Dark Side." *International Journal of Selection and Assessment,* 2001, *9,* 40–51.

Hogan, R., and Hogan, J. "Theoretical Frameworks for Assessment." In P. R. Jeanneret and R. Silzer (eds.), *Individual Assessment.* San Francisco: Jossey-Bass, 1997.

Hogan, R., and Smither, R. *Personality: Theories and Applications.* Boulder, Colo.: Westview Press, 2001.

Hogan, R., Curphy, G., and Hogan, J. "What We Know About Leadership: Effectiveness and Personality." *American Psychologist,* 1994, *51,* 469–477.

Horney, K. *Neurosis and Human Growth.* New York: Norton, 1950.

Katzenbach, J. R. *Teams at the Top.* Boston: Harvard Business School Press, 1998.

Koestenbaum, P. *The Heart of Business: Ethics, Power and Philosophy.* Dallas: Saybrook, 1991.

Kotter, J. P. "Why Transformation Efforts Fail." *Harvard Business Review,* Mar. 1995.

Kouzes, J. M., and Posner, B. Z. *Leadership Challenge.* (3rd ed.) San Francisco: Jossey-Bass, 2002.

Lundin, W., and Lundin, K. *The Healing Manager: How to Build Quality Relationships and Productive Cultures at Work.* San Francisco: Berrett-Koehler, 1993.

Marrs, D. *Executive in Passage: Career in Crisis—the Door to Uncommon Fulfillment.* Los Angeles: Barrington Sky, 1990.

McCall, M. W., Jr., and Lombardo, M. M. "Off the Track: Why and How Successful Executives Get Derailed" (Tech. Rep. no. 21). Greensboro, N.C.: Center for Creative Leadership, 1983.

McCall, M. W., Jr., Lombardo, M. M., and Morrison, A. M. *Lessons of Experience.* Lexington, Mass.: Lexington Press, 1988.

O'Neill, J. R. *The Paradox of Success: When Winning at Work Means Losing at Life—a Book of Renewal for Leaders.* New York: Traches, 1994.

Pearson, C., and Seivert, S. *Magic at Work: Camelot, Creative Leadership, and Everyday Miracles.* New York: Doubleday, 1995.

Pfeffer, J., and Sutton, R. I. *The Knowing-Doing Gap: How Smart Companies Turn Knowledge into Action.* Boston: Harvard Business School Press, 2000.

Quinn, R. E. *Deep Change: Discovering the Leader Within.* San Francisco: Jossey-Bass, 1996.

Roberts, B. W., and Hogan, R. (eds.). *Personality Psychology in the Workplace.* Washington, D.C.: American Psychological Association, 2001.

Shaw, R. B. *Trust in the Balance: Building Successful Organizations on Results, Integrity, and Concern.* San Francisco: Jossey-Bass, 1997.

Sonnenfeld, J. *The Hero's Farewell: What Happens When CEOs Retire.* New York: Oxford University Press, 1988.

Thompson, M. C. *The Congruent Life: Following the Inward Path to Fulfilling Work and Inspired Leadership.* San Francisco: Jossey-Bass, 2000.

Wackerle, F. *Straight Talk About Making Tough CEO Selection Decisions.* San Francisco: Jossey-Bass, 2001.

Ward, A., Bishop, K., and Sonnenfeld, J. "Pyrrhic Victories: The Cost to the Board of Ousting the CEO." *Journal of Organizational Behavior,* 1999, *20,* 767–781.

Weisinger, H. *Emotional Intelligence at Work.* San Francisco: Jossey-Bass, 2000.

Wiggins, J. S. (ed.). *The Five-Factor Model of Personality.* New York: Guilford Press, 1996.

POPULAR PRESS ARTICLES

Auletta, K. "Hollywood vs. Harvey." *New Yorker,* Dec. 2002, pp. 64–81.

Associated Press. "Harassment Claim Gets CEO Fired." *Greensboro News and Record,* June 27, 1996.

Associated Press and Bloomberg News. "HPL Technologies Stock Sinks 71% as CEO Fired." *Los Angeles Times,* July 20, 2002.

Baum, G., Patterson, L., and Schibsted, E. "Why They Fail." *Forbes,* Oct. 7, 1996.

Bianco, A., and Moore, P. "Downfall: The Inside Story of the Management Fiasco at Xerox." *Business Week,* Mar. 5, 2001, p. 82.

Bianco, A., and Lavelle, L. "The CEO Trap: Looking for Superheroes to Deliver Sky-High Growth Ensures Disappointment." *Business Week,* Dec. 11, 2000.

Bruno, M. P. "Optical Cable Chief Executive Fired." *Washington Post,* Dec. 4, 2001.

Byrne, J. A., and Grover, D. "Mattel's Lack of Action Figures." *Business Week,* Feb. 21, 2000.

"Can Miller Put the Oomph Back in AOL?" *Business Week,* Aug. 26, 2002.

Colvin, G. "The Anti-Control Freak: In Ricardo Semler's Company, Workers Pick Their Own Hours and the CEO Has a Temp Job." *Fortune,* Nov. 26, 2001.

Cope, N. "Head of Kingfisher, Geoff Mulcahy . . . Needs to Produce One More Dazzling Trick." *Independent,* London, July 11, 2001.

Crockett, R. "Motorola: Can Chris Galvin Save His Family's Legacy?" *Business Week,* July 16, 2001.

Downey Grimsley, K. "Romances with the Boss Raise Red Flags." *Washington Post,* Jan. 29, 1998.

Elkind, P. "Garbage In Garbage Out." *Fortune,* May 25, 1998.

Ellis, J. "Life After Enron's Death." *Fast Company,* Mar. 2002, pp. 118–120.

Elston, C., and Gabrick, J. J. "S.O.S for High-Tech Mergers and Acquisitions: How to Avoid 'Titanic' Mistakes in Turbulent Waters." Canonsburg, Pa.: MindMatters Technologies, n.d.

Fairlamb, D. "Fallen Star." *Business Week,* Mar. 4, 2002, p. 70.

Fairlamb, D. "Trouble in Paradise." *Business Week,* July 29, 2002, p. 56.

Gaines-Ross, L. "CEOs Stranded in Wonderland: A CEO's Number One Asset Is Credibility, but He or She Doesn't Have Much Time to Build It." *Journal of Business Strategy,* Mar. 1, 2002.

Hall, W. "Swiss Business Star Stumbles at the Top . . ." *Financial Times,* Jan. 30, 2002.

Hanson, L. "What Boards Can Do About America's Corporate Leadership Crisis." *Directorship,* Apr. 1, 2002.

Harrison, M. "Boardroom Coup Ends Messier's Reign at Vivendi." *Independent,* London, July 2, 2002.

Johnson, C. "Thorough Nokia History Has Much to Offer Executives." *Fort Worth Star-Telegram,* July 21, 2001.

Kaufman, L. "After 15 Years, Executive's Short Goodbye." *New York Times,* Nov. 17, 2001.

Labathon, S. "Praise to Scorn: Mercurial Ride of S.E.C. Chief." *Washington Post,* Nov. 10, 2002.

Lucier, C., Spiegel, E., and Schuyt, R. "Why CEOs Fall: The Causes and Consequences of Turnover at the Top." *Strategy + Business,* 2002 (3rd Q.), 28, n.p.

McClenahen, J. "Hit the Road, Jack." *Industry Week,* Mar. 19, 2001.

Miller, M., Clifford, M., and Zegel, S. "Dishonored Dealmaker—an Insider Look at the Rise and Fall of Flamboyant Tycoon J. Ting." *Business Week,* Aug. 12, 2002, p. 44.

Morris, K. "The Rise of Jill Barad." *Business Week,* May 25, 1998.

Naughton, K. "The Mighty Fall: Once They Were Worshiped as Heroes, but Now CEOs Are Being Grilled by Boards . . . " *Newsweek,* Aug. 5, 2002.

O'Harrow, R., and Hilzenrath, D. "Executive Fired in Bank Probe: Money Laundering Inquiry Tries to Track Funds from Russia." *Washington Post,* Aug. 28, 1999.

Race, T. "Like Narcissus, Executives Are Smitten, and Undone, by Their Own Images." *New York Times,* July 29, 2002.

Reuteman, R. "Workers Find Straight Talk from CEOs Hard to Take." *Rocky Mountain News,* Aug. 17, 2002.

Ringshaw, G. "Huppi Falls from His Mountain . . . " *Sunday Telegraph,* London, Mar. 3, 2002, p. 10.

Rosenfeld, J. "Blam! Maximum Success." *Fast Company,* Jan. 2001, p. 127.

Sloane, J. "Corporate Kindness Might Cost Aaron Feuerstein His Family's Mill." Fortune.com, Mar. 1, 2002.

Slocum, J. W., Jr., Ragan, C., and Casey, A. "The Corporate Leadership Capacity of CEOs." *Organizational Dynamics,* 2002, *30*(3), 269–281.

Tomlinson, R. "Dethroning Percy Barnevik." Fortune.com, Apr. 1, 2002.

Wheatcroft, P. "The Human Factor." *Management Today,* Mar. 2002, p. 29.

Wolfson, B. J. "Head of ICN Pharmaceuticals in Costa Mesa, California, to Resign." *Orange County Register,* June 19, 2002.

ACKNOWLEDGMENTS

It is impossible to write a book on derailment and acknowledge others without somehow implying they may know the topic too well. We don't want to create that perception. But we do want to thank a number of people whose authenticity and openness with us have contributed to our understanding of the complexity of leadership life and whose contributions run throughout this book.

In the course of working with outstanding leaders, we have witnessed how their self-knowledge, honesty, and openness to learning have contributed to their performance. Some of these leaders include Bill Weldon, Andrea Jung, Kerry Killinger, Reuben Mark, John Hammergren, Sidney Taurel, Ray Gilmartin, Ken Lewis, Bob Glynn, Craig Barrett, Dan Vasella, Joe Tucci, Scott McNealy, Brian Hall, and Duane Ackerman. None of them are referenced in these pages.

To discuss and understand the dark side that resides in all of us, we are especially fortunate to have many people who masquerade as clients and colleagues but who in fact are good friends, who work hard at being both leaders and genuine human beings. Those we especially want to thank are Norman Walker, Anish Batlaw, Per Peterson, Barbara Hurtig, Bill McComb, Chris Poon, Roger Fine, Mike Carey, Russ Deyo, Brian Perkins, Bob Joy, Allan Weisberg, Barbara Elbertson, Susan Weir, Deborrah Himsel, Jill Kanin-Lovers, Susan Kropf, Bob Corti, Pat Gelsinger, Greg

Matsunami, Antoine Tirard, Frank Waltmann, Jean Brennan, Brent Stanley, Jordan Wand, Ethan Hanabury, Jaki Sitterle, Bill Klepper, Mike Fenlon, Dave Jennings, Mindy Grossman, Linda Clark-Santos, Pam Layton, Charley Corace, Allie Mysliwy, Laura Dorsey, Lisa Cheraskin, Brent Stanley, Michael McNamara, Suzy Herivel Maloney, Mary Jean Conners, Jack Mullen, Melody Richards, Christian Dellekoenig, Patti Lewis, Rafael de la Garza, Jean Brennan, Wes Coleman, Fernando Mendez, Judy Braun, Val Markos, Eva Sage-Gavin, Jim Sutton, Jim Shanley, Kevin Kendrick, Steele Alphin, Crawford Beveridge, Brenda Bluemke, Joe Rose, Lynn Badaracco, Mark Mula, Grey Warner, Bob Mann, Howard Levine, Melanie Cadenhead, Corey Seitz, Daniele Joudene, Chris Bober, and Sandy Flynn.

The principals, experts, and coaches of the CDR International network routinely challenge us to think deeper and differently, and we value their insights and support. Some of these include Jim Noel, Neil Johnston, Deborah Barber, Alice Portz, Ron Meeks, Susan Dunn, Jill Conner, Mark Kiefaber, Carole France, John Bradberry, Ginny Whitelaw, Rod Anderson, Neville Osrin, Peg Howell, Valerie Waters, Mike Fruge, Ralph Bates, Charles Brassard, Paula Chronister, Peter Tattle, Terry O'Connor, and Lars Cederholm.

Susan Williams of Jossey-Bass envisioned this book and supported the project with ideas, critiques, and deadlines. At CDR International, several people deserve special thanks: Amy Nielsen for her diligent research; Steffie Armontrout for overseeing the final editing; Brenda Fogelman, Marisol Cadiz, and Judy Ray who help keep us from derailing; Richard Aldersea, who reminds us we have a business to run; Stephen Rhinesmith, our partner, who makes it fun and worth doing; and the entire CDR International staff, who make us proud to be part of the organization.

Our families have also supported the many nights away, phone calls during vacations, and long hours in front of the computer necessary to complete this book: Doug, Carter, and Jeremy; and Kathy, Danielle, Justin, and Megan. Their love and support make it all possible and worthwhile.

February 2003

David L. Dotlich
Portland, Oregon

Peter C. Cairo
Bearsville, New York

ABOUT THE AUTHORS
AND CDR INTERNATIONAL

David L. Dotlich, Ph.D., has been involved with planned organizational change in academics, business, government, and consulting for twenty years. He was formerly executive vice president of Honeywell International and Groupe Bull. David is a business adviser and coach to senior executives of Johnson & Johnson, Bank of America, McKesson, Merck, Novartis, Intel, Washington Mutual, and many others. He is the coauthor of *Action Learning* (Jossey-Bass, 1998), *Action Coaching* (Jossey-Bass, 1999), and *Unnatural Leadership: Going Against Intuition and Experience to Develop Ten New Leadership Instincts* (Jossey-Bass, 2002).

Peter C. Cairo, Ph.D., is a consultant who specializes in the areas of leadership development, executive coaching, and organization effectiveness. He is the former chair of the Department of Organizational and Counseling Psychology at Columbia University and currently a member of the faculty of Columbia University Business School Executive Education. Peter's clients include Avon Products, Merck, Colgate, Bank of America, Lilly, and Thomson. He is the coauthor of *Action Coaching* (Jossey-Bass, 1999), and *Unnatural Leadership: Going Against Intuition and Experience to Develop Ten New Leadership Instincts* (Jossey-Bass 2002).

CDR International is a global consulting firm that specializes in top-tier in-house coaching, consulting, and executive education programs. Both authors are partners in the firm, along with Stephen Rhinesmith, Ph.D., and they work in partnership with Columbia University Business School Executive Education to deliver Action Learning and Action Coaching programs that corporations use as a strategic lever to develop global business leaders, integrate acquisitions, transform organizations, and grow businesses.

CDR International also offers two public programs. "Leading for the Long Term," developed in partnership with Canyon Ranch Health Resort, helps senior executives identify new ways to live healthy lives while leading effectively, developing new sources of energy, and responding flexibly and creatively to the needs of work, family, and community. "High Impact Human Resource Leadership" is a two-week Action Learning executive program delivered twice each year for a consortium of six companies who send a team of senior HR executives.

CDR International's Executive Action Learning and Action Coaching programs promote business and leadership performance improvement through real-time business problem solving, individual assessments (including the CDR International Leadership Derailment Survey), and one-on-one coaching. CDR International's executive leadership programs provide executives with business and leadership skills needed to lead organizations in the uncertain environment and economy of the twenty-first century. To learn more about how your company can implement executive leadership programs—or to learn more about CDR International itself—visit http://www.cdr-intl.com. Or you may contact CDR International directly:

CDR International
120 NW 9th Avenue, Suite 216
Portland, Oregon 97209
Phone: 503-223-5678 (twenty-four hours)
Fax: 503-223-5677

INDEX